The Mindfulness Sidekick

The Mindfulness Sidekick

Mental Wellness to Maximize Transcranial Magnetic Stimulation

AMY HALLORAN-STEINER, LCSW

Copyright © 2021 by Amy Halloran-Steiner

All rights reserved. No part of this book may be reproduced or used in any manner without written permission of the copyright owner except in the case of brief quotations embodied in critical articles and reviews.

ISBN 978-1-7368993-0-4

Also available as an ebook: 978-1-7368993-1-1

The material in this book should, in no way, substitute for professional mental health or medical doctor care. The author is not directly affiliated with any TMS treatment or TMS product and does not propose to opine on the subject beyond what is contained in this edition.

*This book is dedicated to those who are seeking
a better way to be and who are willing to let go of judgment,
to be present and to acknowledge what IS.
May we let life live through us with peace and ease.*

Contents

Foreword	1
Preface	3
Introduction	5
TMS Week Zero: Getting Ready	17
TMS Week One: Starting Out	31
TMS Week Two: Accepting This Human Brain	55
TMS Week Three: Knowing the Mind and Being in The Body	71
TMS Week Four: Summoning Gratitude	91
TMS Week Five: Being Whole and a Part of a System	105
TMS Week Six: Acting Discerningly, Communicating Compassionately	119
TMS Week Seven: Cultivating Loving-Kindness	141
TMS Week Eight: Scheduling Your Time	151
TMS Week Nine: Strengthening Mindfulness and Your Life	165
Notes	179
Resources	191
Acknowledgments	199
About the Author	201

Foreword

Amy Halloran-Steiner is a licensed clinical social worker, certified alcohol and drug counselor, mindfulness instructor and a farmer who is on a mission to connect individuals to themselves, to one another, and to the earth, for maximum well-being for all. You're holding in your hands the work of a person with the passion, dedication and expertise to help you live your best life.

While walking among the trees on her farm one afternoon, Amy and I had a thrilling brainstorm about mindfulness, nature, movement, TMS and all the ways we could combine research-based treatment and our passion for helping others into the superpower of all superpower tools of healing!

We marveled at the human capacity for healing and how mindfulness and TMS could intersect to create even greater well-being for those we serve. We joked that we could bring my Transcranial Magnetic Stimulation equipment out to her woods, meditate, hug some trees, sing campfire songs. . .

But, alas, the equipment weighs 500 pounds, neither of us had a flatbed truck, and there was the reality of liability to contend with. So, we compromised on the idea that Amy would create a mindfulness program tailored to follow folks as they engage in TMS treatment.

A person can't have these kinds of fantastical conversations with just anyone. These are the kinds of impassioned discussions that come easy with Amy because she is a creative risk-taker, a humble intellectual, a dedicated steward of our planet and its inhabitants, a dreamer, a doer, an expert therapist and mindfulness instructor, and an overall engaged and compassionate human. Amy carries a refreshing sense of wonder and humor that permeates her life and work.

Many people ask, what the heck is TMS? TMS—Transcranial Magnetic Stimulation—is a non-drug FDA-approved treatment for depression. It involves placing a small but powerful magnet on the head, which creates an electrical field that stimulates brain cells involved in mood regulation. Repetitive stimulation of these brain cells rehabilitates neural networks that are dysfunctional in depression. Research tells us that TMS is highly effective for at least 70% of people and indeed, in my clinic, we have witnessed nothing short of miracles—lives changed, families strengthened, dreams recovered, and hope restored.

Why the combination of mindfulness and TMS? There is ample evidence that regular mindfulness practice leads to measurable changes in the brain, improved resilience, mood regulation, and overall well-being (not to mention a host of other measurable health benefits). TMS + mindfulness has the capacity for a synergistic and compounded positive effect on neural plasticity which can result in remission of depression and overall enhanced sense of well-being.

This book is vital because it stands to help the millions of people who are desperately seeking a way out of depression. A person can also reap the lessons of *The Mindfulness Sidekick* on its own, without TMS treatment. Each chapter teaches important concepts related to mindfulness and living a healthy life that would support anyone seeking relief from suffering.

The Mindfulness Sidekick is not only a book; it also bestows access to a rich YouTube Playlist of yoga sessions, guided meditations, and helpful teachings that support you along your healing journey. It's like having a live teacher at your disposal. Amy's friendly, accepting demeanor acts as a gentle yet expert guide to lead you in your practice of self-discovery and healing.

I hope to see Amy write more *Mindfulness Sidekick* guidebooks for other challenges people face on this journey to their most meaningful, most fulfilled life. This book has the potential to dramatically change your life. How you utilize this powerful tool is up to you!

Jennifer Behnke
Board Certified Psychiatric Mental Health Nurse Practitioner
Clinical TMS Society Member

Preface

The Mindfulness Sidekick you now hold in your hands is a labor of love. As a licensed clinical social worker, therapist, mindfulness teacher and practitioner, I have grown to love the delightful epiphanies that come from paying attention on purpose to what is already happening inside of and around me. I love recognizing patterns in my own life that open up possibilities for gratitude and change. I love the startled realizations of students who, upon hearing something explained with the right combination of words, recognize themselves in what they've just experienced. I love how every human being can awaken to life when they merely pause. So simple, this awakening, and yet so almost out of reach, lending itself to a divine experience brought about by not talking, striving, nor judging. It's as if we hold out our hand, and in our stillness, a tiny bird lands on our fingers for the briefest of moments. My mission is to encourage folks to hold out their hands and invite that small timid bird to come, her skinniest of stick-legs stopping there to remind us that we are worthy of waking up to life's realness.

Life is often *not* beautiful. It is painful and can break our hearts over and over, but I have learned it's better to break my own heart than to be walking around in the cocooned life of denial, while my thoughts reproduce themselves, treading upon the fresh grass of this new moment, my body giving me messages that I neither acknowledge nor act on for my own best health. No, I choose to be awake to this world and to open my heart to all that it endows in me, building skills to work with whatever comes, in order to truly be alive.

I teamed up with Jennifer Behnke, Psychiatric-Mental Health Nurse Practitioner (PMHNP), to provide the highest quality of mental wellness support to participants of Transcranial Magnetic Stimulation, a promising non-invasive treatment for severe depression, obsessive compulsive disorder (OCD), post-traumatic stress disorder (PTSD) and a handful of other conditions. These conditions rob people of their chance to walk the path to their richest, most purposeful lives. We have endeavored to create a compound solution that works for people, not just to solve their mental health challenge, but to give them tools to cope with the full range of challenges throughout their lives.

May you, Readers, interact with this book and feel my warm presence reminding you that brain change with the help of mindfulness is not only possible, but can be delightful. May you move from the afflictions of the mind toward an awakeness that not only supports your wellness, but also opens your heart and connects you vitally to what is most important to you. I invite you to join in the revolution of becoming mindful one breath, one page, one day at a time. With this book, I wish for you the blessing of those days, full of the whole host of joys, sorrows, wants and gifts. May you enjoy a sacred relationship with all your inner experiences as they pass through the vastness, goodness and wholeness that is you. You deserve mindful awareness; welcome to the path to your most meaningful life.

Introduction

"No one saves us but ourselves. No one can and no one may. We ourselves must walk the path."

—GAUTAMA BUDDHA

Introducing The Mindfulness Sidekick

Finally, here is a helpful resource to use as you embark on this journey to change your brain and improve your mental health. *The Mindfulness Sidekick* is your guidebook from the very beginning of your commitment to Transcranial Magnetic Stimulation (TMS) all the way through the last week of active treatment. Beyond treatment, you'll be able to use *The Mindfulness Sidekick* for as long as you choose mindfulness to help you relate to the ups and downs of life. Both TMS and mindfulness are powerful influences propelling you along your own unique path to a richer, healthier, more fulfilling life.

Repetition Is Key To Brain Change

Just as you practiced multiplication tables in school or piano scales at home when you were younger, you will be asked to practice mindfulness exercises over and over again. Brain research shows that repetition makes lasting brain change, and mindfulness practice certainly grows best with reps. TMS has been shown to change the structure of your brain, and a consistent mindfulness practice adds important prefrontal cortex stimulation that grows your capacity for clarity and acceptance, leading the way to your own long-term mental wellness.

Weeks 0-9

The next chapter, entitled **Week Zero,** readies you the week before TMS treatment starts by expanding your basic understanding of mindfulness, so that you will be prepared to use mindfulness when you sit in the TMS chair the first day of **Week One**.

By **Week Nine**—generally the week of your last scheduled TMS treatment—you will have had a chance to practice more than 9 different skills and more than a dozen variations on those skills that invite mindfulness into the ways you generally move through your life. If this list below feels overwhelming, can you notice that experience without judgment? The great Chinese philosopher Lao Tzu said, "The journey of a thousand miles begins with the first step." You have taken a powerful first step by signing up for TMS treatment and a second one by buying this book and reading this first chapter. These steps are choices that perhaps come from some deep knowing of what you need to heal, and I commend you for having acted on that knowing. May it pay off abundantly.

What to Expect in Each Chapter

You'll see the following in each chapter of *The Mindfulness Sidekick*:

"EXPERIENCE" will summarize briefly what other participants have shared of their experience in TMS treatment at that stage of treatment. You'll see that the variety of experiences is wide, and changes happen at different paces. If you ever have questions about your own experience, please talk with your TMS treatment team. *This section will be untitled, first in each chapter and in italics.*

"UNDERSTANDING" introduces new concepts for understanding how to weave mindful acceptance and commitment to change into your own personal TMS treatment as well as into your life beyond treatment.

"SKILL TO TRY" is a formal mindfulness practice that helps build your capacity for awareness. Each skill is explained briefly in the book, and then you will be guided through the activity on the Mindfulness Sidekick YouTube Playlist, accessed on your phone, tablet or computer. Find the access info in the notes for this Introduction chapter. These skills are important building blocks to your wellness.

"HOME PRACTICE" is your homework, which can be done at any point in the day or week. It is structure for those reps that will change your brain for the better. Through HOME PRACTICE, you will transform into a practitioner of mindfulness; willingness and commitment are the home practitioner's best allies. Again, you'll want to access your YouTube Playlist.

"WRITING REFLECTION" is a chance for you to synthesize important observations and epiphanies that come to you on this journey to wellness. You can fill in the spaces in this book or keep your own journal if that works better for you. There are extra pages in the back to write additional reflections on this journey.

"NATURE CONNECTION" is a short nature-based activity that invites you to bring attention to your own connection with the natural world, opening your senses to the healing that nature offers. Research shows that access to nature calms the nervous system and clears the way for new growth and discovery.

"WISE WORDS" round out each chapter to open your mind to someone else's wisdom and perspective.

What you have in your hands is only one part of *The Mindfulness Sidekick*; as mentioned, you have also received vital access to the private Mindfulness Sidekick's YouTube Playlist so that you can learn by doing. You will be able to cultivate a mindfulness practice of your own as you choose your pace. You'll learn to tune in and to let go. You can decide which activities bring you ease and clarity, which practices increase your motivation and which help you take good care of yourself as you commit again and again to improving your mental well-being. Perhaps you'll be using this and other mindfulness instruction for years to come, as you change and grow and develop into the future self about whom you dream. See Introduction notes for access to the YouTube Playlist.

Self-Care

You have already made a significant time and financial commitment to TMS treatment. By taking part in *the Mindfulness Sidekick*, you will maximize your ability to head toward the life you want. This journey of change toward a desired life of well-being goes most directly when the traveler achieves balance along the way. It will be essential that you not strive so hard that you create more stress in your life and that, at the same time, you challenge yourself to keep practicing, even when you have thoughts that pressure you to stop. This is another opportunity to notice the thoughts, emotions and sensations pressuring you to sabotage all this progress. Instead, you'll follow the practices and prompts to navigate your own path to your best life.

Please take good care of yourself as you learn more about mindfulness; along the way, you can care for your body by eating well, making quiet time to sleep, getting exercise and fresh air, and dealing with some of your stressors. You can nurture your emotional and spiritual self by gathering support around you and by staying in touch with the forces outside of you that help you tune into safety, meaning and even the divine in your own life. You might choose at least one vital, trusted support person who will be with you along the way. This person should be ready to listen, comfort, provide feedback, help trouble-shoot, and cheer you on as you progress on this path.

Just as a distance hiker would never approach their desired destination with no support, too-small boots, two hours of sleep, only Tootsie Rolls for food and no hope of ever arriving at the destination, you will do best on this journey by doing the behaviors that help you thrive and head you toward your most desired future self.

There will be plenty of other help along this learning path; in addition to the loved ones you already know, your TMS treatment team is ready to help you. For the duration of your treatment, these folks will be present to celebrate when you persist through something that is difficult or when you can actually enjoy something on your path. Please look around you, as well, for those natural helpers in your life that want to be part of your change. It's too much to expect you'll change your brain all alone!

Mindfulness, Our Featured Guest and Teacher

Mindfulness is the science-based practice of paying purposeful attention to the present moment nonjudgmentally. **Awareness** is the presence of mind that happens naturally when you are paying attention in this special way. There is evidence that a regular mindfulness practice reduces stress,[1] reduces anxiety levels,[2] improves symptoms of depression,[3] decreases inflammatory chemicals contributing to depression symptoms,[4] and can increase sleep.[5] Whew! All that, by just paying better attention? Well, yes, it's that simple *and* at the same time, it's a difficult action to do regularly.

When you pay attention on purpose, nonjudgmentally to what the present moment is bringing you, you are cultivating mindfulness and you can more easily:

- notice the thinking and choose to focus on something in the here and now instead of being mesmerized by thoughts, caught in suffering or shut down altogether;
- be present enough to appreciate the small pleasures of your day;
- accept what's happening without trying to fix it, all the while acting on your values and moving in the direction of the life you want;
- relate to and deal with difficult emotions and mood states that bestow themselves upon all humans;
- catch the downward spiral of a bad mood or difficult memory to then work at changing your own experience;
- release attention from the mostly negative to be less judgmental and convert to a more balanced perspective;
- bring enough friendliness to yourself and have confidence to do hard things;
- abide inner experiences with calm and persevere on the path to your purposeful life.

An ongoing mindfulness practice can change the brain to support more present focus, less rumination about the past and less worry about the future. When we repeat brain-helpful actions like TMS, meditation, yoga and well-timed psychotherapy, we change the structure of the brain, thus in turn, transforming the way the mind functions. Then your own experience of thoughts, feelings and sensations that lead you to actions can change for the better, and your choice of actions can improve, contributing to your better life.

While it's easy to *explain* mindfulness, it takes considerable effort to *achieve* consistent mindfulness because our brains constantly drag our attention away from the present moment; and when our brain *does* let our attention land in the now, our thoughts can be judgy and negative. There are evolutionary reasons your brain keeps successfully escaping from present moment awareness, but this tendency is now mostly unwarranted, because you are likely not living a life like your long-ago ancestors in which they needed to be super-cautious about threats which require fighting, freezing or fleeing in an instant, with no technology to mitigate discomfort or threat. If you are in constant threat of cougars about to pounce, hurricanes brewing in the close skies and no shelter at hand, or enemy tribal warriors running your way, then you need a different sort of book and mindfulness is not your best tool.

We are lucky that our brains (and specifically our amygdalas) do not need to be so on guard for fighting, fleeing or freezing all the time. Some people have had such difficult experiences previously, however, that their brains act with a hair trigger to keep their bodies safe. Some people's experience has conditioned their brains to be so sensitive to detecting every calamity that could go wrong because they *did* have to send a message to their body to save them at some point(s). If you suspect that this is the case for you, that previous trauma has gotten your brain too conditioned for danger, then please share this with your TMS treatment provider. They may discuss with you adjustments that can be made in treatment to better facilitate the process of rehabilitating this adaptive tendency of your brain. There are also many actions you can take to assist your brain in relearning what is safety and what is danger and to smooth out the difficult inner experiences you might still be having as a result of things in the past, or possibly even things happening currently.

Our best lives usually involve a good measure of feeling calm, safe and confident in the world around us, so when we can, we practice mindfulness to build the pathways to create that delicious safety. When we feel secure, we can act to embody the joy that is available to us and keep behaving in our own healthiest best interest. First, we need to create that safety, and it's usually much easier with a support team, so please speak to your TMS treatment provider or a therapist who is trained in the treatment of trauma to help you to use the resources you have inside of and around you. If you feel panicked or unsafe at any time throughout the course of your TMS treatment, please tell your TMS provider immediately. It is not necessary or advisable to "muscle through" these intense and scary feelings.[6]

TMS and Mindfulness

Transcranial Magnetic Stimulation and a mindfulness practice together give you a chance to take back a bit of control over the brain's negativity bias ("Hey, my person," says your brain's limbic system, "I'm sure something's about to go badly wrong! Watch out!") and to *enjoy* (literally "bring joy into the body") the benefits of safety in the life you can lead. You'll be invited early on to understand what's important to you and to imagine a better way of living.

TMS invites those tiny brain cells to reproduce and thereby create healthy pathways to change and heal from depression. Mindfulness invites you to get curious about what you experience every moment. Throughout each day, you can notice what you experience, label that experience and leave it alone because another experience is sure to come on its heels! Once you know the patterns to your experiences, you can gain clarity about making better choices to create the life you want. Let's do this!

What Are We Accepting When It Comes To Depression?

First, let's reckon with *what actually is,* related to depression. You have likely chosen TMS treatment because you detest the fistful of symptoms you've experienced with depression that you'd like to drop on the ground and walk away from. Which of these are part of your "*what actually is*"?

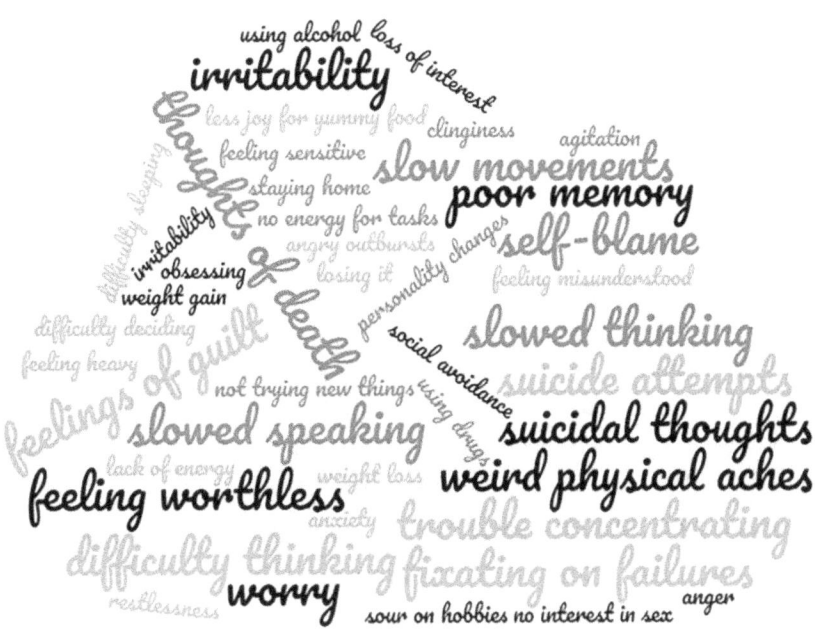

When you accept the symptoms of depression, you are not passively admitting it will always be like this. Rather, you are acknowledging that these symptoms have been a part of your experience and from there, you will make choices to move in a direction that matters to you. All of the above depression symptoms are at once normal and transmutable. No matter how influential these symptoms have been in your experience lately, they can go away, especially with your efforts.

To achieve some measure of acceptance, it helps some people to imagine that they are vast like the sky and that these symptoms—as well as their difficult thoughts, overwhelmingly uncomfortable feelings, and incredibly bothersome physical experiences—can pass through them like clouds pass through the open blue sky. No matter how clogged with clouds the sky is at any point, we all know that there is still clear blue above. While this doesn't make the experiences go away, it might give you a sense of openness to change rather than a stuck sense of powerlessness to rid yourself of depression.

Showing Up with Mindfulness

Despite the many limiting symptoms you have experienced, you have attained the victory of bravely showing up to TMS treatment, taking the steps on this path toward a life of consistent meaning, purpose, and joy. As theoretical physicist and author Stephen Hawking said, "Half the battle is just showing up."

Every life has stress and sadness. When you show up to what's happening and pay attention without judging yourself, you will likely experience unhelpful thoughts, emotions and sensations, and you might *nevertheless* build the muscles of focus that will lead to new ways of navigating stressful situations. This is the help *The Mindfulness Sidekick* has to offer.

How TMS Contributes to Wellness

As you likely know, TMS improves symptoms of depression by stimulating and repairing groups of brain cells called neural networks in the regions of the brain involved in mood control. You can think of TMS as rehab for your brain. In the same way that physical therapy can repair an injury through repetitive stretches and exercises, TMS repairs damaged or sluggish neural networks through repetitive activation. As the saying goes, "neurons that fire together wire together," meaning the more often a neural network is activated, the stronger it becomes. TMS improves depression by retraining your brain cells to work together.

While TMS has been shown to be highly effective in reducing or eliminating depression, you will still have a brain that churns out millions of thoughts each week, a body that feels fear and a heart that mourns and regrets. Mindfulness will help you relate with all those parts of being human that cause suffering, so that you might suffer less and thrive more.

The Mindfulness Sidekick teams up with TMS to support you in walking your path toward the life that you want to lead, a life that is richer, more meaningful and more packed with all the good stuff that awaits you. You are not alone; there are others on similar paths nearby and there is much help along the way. Let's get started!

TMS Week Zero

"Fear is just excitement without the breath."

—FRITZ PERLS, MD

Getting Ready

Many people start their journey through Transcranial Magnetic Stimulation long before they sit in the chair for the first session. They usually experience years of depressed mood as they become convinced that depression is something about them, either a weakness, a choice, or a curse. Usually, they just want depression to stop. They then might learn about TMS and think "could I do this treatment?" This thought might lead to hope and excitement with the thought "could this be the thing that works for me?" but then maybe terror floods in with something like, "Am I totally broken and unable to be mended? What if I try and it fails and I know I am completely broken?" Or maybe there is a reasonable thought of "No, depression is very common, I just have a bad case of it and new science does help people" which brings worry and, "What if I'm the only one that science cannot help? What if I am immune to even TMS?" and back and forth, up and down the thoughts and the feelings go.

Can you remember your own version of this roller coaster inside? OK, take a breath. That's it—a deep breath—and let it out slowly. Good. Now, let's start with an acknowledgement of *what is*.

Understanding

Anticipating Your Journey with TMS and Mindfulness

You have already made it through some of the most difficult steps. You found a TMS provider amidst the many provider options, read the shiny materials, scheduled an appointment, told your life story to a stranger, learned about the science behind TMS, debated about whether this was right for you, talked about it with supportive others, did some calculations about whether you could afford the money and the time, maybe even went into deep reflection about it or prayed about it. And you said "Yes." Your choice to dedicate valuable resources toward your future self, to be changed by this treatment, is important to acknowledge. You have committed to show up every weekday for many weeks. That's no short amount of time; did you know that three litters of rabbits can be born from the same mother in the nine weeks you'll be in treatment? And then you must know (so as not to waste your money) that to some degree, you'll have to maintain the positive changes that your commitment to TMS brings with some planned healthy living. Yes, you identified your values and you went for it. When you get to the place in this book where you are asked to identify your values, please consider that commitment, persistence, and perseverance are values that you are already living into.

It makes sense, then, after a significant amount of time hosting those nasty depression symptoms, and then committing to three whole litters of rabbits and enough money to feed a whole fluffle of rabbits, that you are probably having lots of thoughts and feelings about the first day of your TMS treatment. Perhaps you have the thought that you don't like to start new things (feeling nervous, tentative), or perhaps you are having the thought that TMS might really help you (feeling hopeful, excited). Those thoughts and feelings are obviously linked and related even if you aren't sure which came first. With all these inner experiences happening in anticipation of Day 1, if you slow down, you might be able to note some sensations in your body, too. Perhaps the feeling of nervousness brings a tightness in the chest or a fluttering in the stomach; perhaps hopefulness brings a sense of lightness and openness in the shoulders and back. Taking some time to be present and to acknowledge *what is* is exactly the journey we are on together. There are no wrong answers, only experiences you notice.

With persistence and commitment, you'll learn to turn your attention to what's happening inside of you and to understand more about yourself and about how you can awaken to the true experience of the present moment.

Keep in mind that mindfulness practice for depression is not about experiential control. It's not about making depression go away, leading to only happiness. This practice of mindfulness is about being more present in your own life so that you can relate to whatever comes in a new way and so that you bring all your personal resources and strengths to the actual living of this life. In this way, with awakeness and awareness, you can use the experience of depression to jumpstart your journey on the path to your richest, most purposeful life.

What Mindfulness Is and Is Not

So let's understand that mindfulness. . .

- is not an escape, but a way to see more clearly;
- is not designed to make those depressed feelings and thoughts go away; TMS is designed to do that! You may start to notice that you are having fewer depressed thoughts and feelings as your mindfulness practices get stronger and you may be awake enough to enjoy that noticing;
- is helpful in developing your capacity to respond and relate to depression symptoms on this journey as an imperfect human being with a sometimes unhelpful human brain;
- is most helpful when you see the depression as it is, including its impact, and take action based on your values, even if depression is disadvantaging you in the moment.

Nine Attitudes of Mindfulness

Being faithful to your TMS protocol will help diminish depression, and being loyal and dependable in a regular mindfulness practice will help you cope with most of whatever comes. What follows are nine attitudes of mindfulness that support a mindful practice:[1]

Patience, trust, acceptance, letting go, non-striving, nonjudging, beginner's mind, generosity, and **gratitude**.

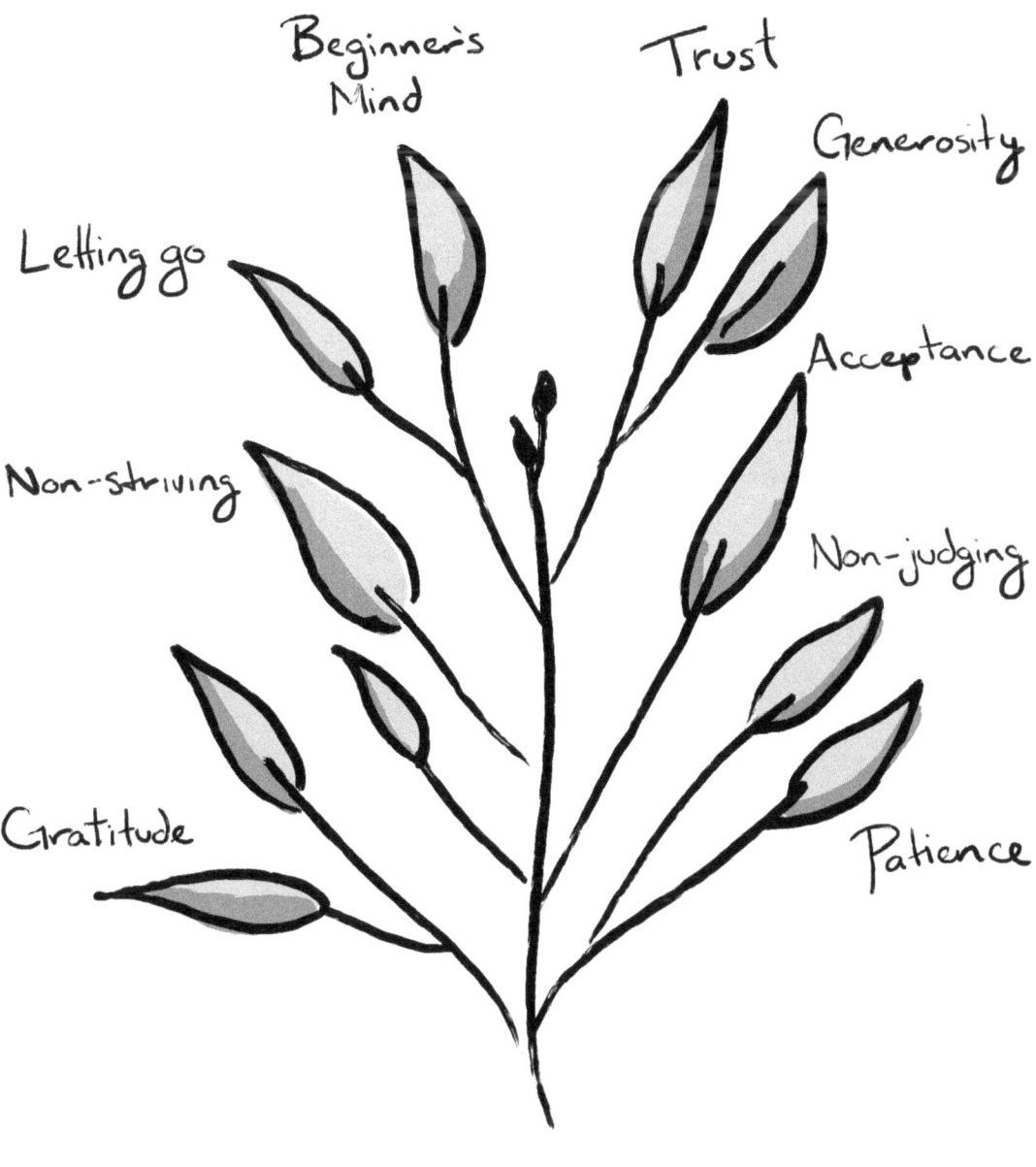

For a more comprehensive look at these attitudes, see the first note in Week Zero Notes.

Skills to Try

Skill One: Raisin Meditation.

This is an introduction to experiencing mindfulness and a chance to practice mindful eating. The Raisin Meditation introduces you to a small morsel and engages your beginner's mind to partake in a new way, without preconceived notions of what you are eating, so that you can more fully experience eating. Find the guided practice on The Mindfulness Sidekick Playlist.

Skill Two: 5 Senses Tour.

This guided practice takes you on a tour of your five senses to experience the world around you in its present moment form, as you probably do very infrequently. Find this guided tour on The Mindfulness Sidekick Playlist.

Home Practice

Do the Raisin Meditation with some morsel of food each day. Expand this practice to your meals as you are able. Eat more foods slowly and mindfully, keeping your attention on what is in your hand or mouth and how you are relating to it. This practice can lead to healthier choices of food and to better digestion, not to mention more time spent at a table, feeling grateful for what you have to eat.

Take the 5 Senses Tour each day and try to incorporate your five senses into more of your experience in your regular life as it flows.

Spend at least five minutes each day remembering why you are committing to TMS and why you have read this far into *The Mindfulness Sidekick*, what values you hold related to recovery from depression. Think specifically about how you want your life to be better and be detailed about your path to a more meaningful life. Write as much of it down as is helpful. There is space at the back of the workbook for you to write.

Writing Reflection

Spend the time you can this week reflecting and writing down your answers to the questions below. Since your main task is to notice, perhaps you can notice when you are pushing yourself too hard to produce writing, and just take your time. This is a new phase in your life's journey and there is no pace you must keep. The week segments are just a suggested structure; it's your book and your time frame.

What did you notice during the first Raisin Meditation? How is this different from how you normally relate to raisins? How might this help you improve your mental well-being?

_____
_____
_____
_____
_____
_____

I chose to do Transcranial Magnetic Stimulation because I intend to:

_____
_____
_____
_____
_____

I'm changing my life around to do TMS by:

_____
_____
_____

I hope that from TMS treatment I:

_____
_____
_____

Specifically, I might be doing the following if depression weren't playing such a predominant role in my life:

_____
_____
_____
_____

Some of the things I'd see, hear, smell, taste or touch regardless of depression's hold on me are:

_____
_____
_____
_____

In order to have a rich, meaningful, purposeful life, I have a goal I want to accomplish. My goal related to depression is:

_____
_____
_____
_____

My needs/values that brought me to TMS are: (see next page)

_____
_____
_____
_____

Values or Needs

Compassionate Communication's Inventory of Needs/Values

CONNECTION
- acceptance
- belonging
- closeness
- compassion
- empathy
- love
- respect/self-respect
- stability
- to see and be seen
- warmth
- affection
- cooperation
- community
- consideration
- inclusion
- mutuality
- safety
- support
- to understand and be understood
- appreciation
- communication
- companionship
- consistency
- intimacy
- nurturing
- security
- to know and be known
- trust

PHYSICAL WELL-BEING
- air
- rest/sleep
- shelter
- food
- sexual expression
- touch
- movement/exercise
- safety
- water

HONESTY
- authenticity
- integrity
- presence

PLAY
- joy
- humor

PEACE
- beauty
- equality
- order
- communion
- harmony
- ease
- inspiration

More Values/Needs

AUTONOMY
- choice
- space
- freedom
- spontaneity
- independence

MEANING
- awareness
- clarity
- contribution
- efficacy
- hope
- participation
- stimulation
- celebration of life
- competence
- creativity
- effectiveness
- learning
- purpose
- to matter
- challenge
- consciousness
- discovery
- growth
- mourning
- self-expression
- understanding

© NonviolentCommunication.com

Nature Connection

To accompany your sensual experiences this week, take a smell tour of your natural surroundings. Find something that smells, look at it and its habitat for about 10 seconds, and then close your eyes and smell. Some parts of nature are less odiferous, but you can always try to find smelly natural things by scratch-and-sniffing or dig-and-whiffing. If you aren't ready to go outside, then spend the time with your spices, first looking up what each spice looks like as a plant, spending 10 seconds imagining it growing in its natural environment and then closing your eyes and smelling the spice. Notice what happens in your visual space with eyes closed. Notice what happens in the body with your nose open. Consider how this differs from how you normally experience nature. Add these ponderings to your journal, if you like.

Wise Words

The Oracle at Delphi—the spiritual center of the ancient Greek world—gave this simple and famous advice: "Know thyself."

Spiritual teachers like Hellenistic philosopher in Roman Egypt Plotinus (204–270AD) took The Oracle at Delphi's suggestion seriously and urged his students and followers to "Withdraw into yourself and look" and to "close your eyes and invoke a new manner of seeing, a wakefulness that is the birthright of us all, though few put it to use."

TMS Week One

"A year from now, you will wish you had started today."

—KAREN LAMB

"There is nothing more important to true growth than realizing that you are not the voice of the mind — you are the one who hears it."

—MICHAEL SINGER

Starting Out

TMS treatment has begun, and change is magnetic! During Week One, many participants are adjusting to attending daily appointments in the TMS chair and getting used to the sensation of the magnetic coil; each person experiences treatment differently, and so it will be helpful to notice—but not get attached to—the thoughts that might come up about whether you are being strong enough, whether you are too wimpy and whether treatment will feel like this through the whole 9 weeks! You can notice your thinking and try as best you can to come back to your present experience, whether focused on the sensation at the coil, or maybe more helpfully, focused on something more pleasant that is happening in the moment. Can you watch the screen in your TMS office, focus on listening intently to the conversation you are having with your TMS technician? Clients sometimes imagine that they are the bright blue sky mentioned in the introduction, relaxing their body and letting all the discomfort and unwanted emotions pass cleanly through them as they sit in the chair. Others synchronize their breath with the machine, breathing in with the chime and releasing an out-breath when the magnet is pulsing.

TMS participants describe the experience of Week One as not much of anything, slightly uncomfortable, unsettling, painful, or very painful (a low percentage, and in the first days only.) You might notice that you "go away" in your mind when the magnet starts. This is OK, and likely a way your brain has adapted to protect you during painful experiences. You might notice if you are having thoughts that convince you that every session will be equally painful. In TMS, your experience will change over time and it's important to stay open to that possibility. Remember the words of Heraclitus, "The only constant in life is change," and when worry and aversion arise this week, make sure you just keep showing up. Many participants have the thought that, like attempts at treating depression in the past, this new thing won't help either. Some participants also notice feelings of willingness, eagerness, even excitement for TMS. Using the attitudes of patience, trust and non-striving, in this session and beyond, you can keep your mind from getting too far ahead of the present moment and you can treat yourself gently, trusting that you are doing what's best for you. You can talk with your TMS team about any of your experiences in the chair. If there is anything that causes you to feel overwhelmed, please do tell your team.

Understanding

Graphic Change Inside the Brain

Please remember that TMS is already beginning to rehabilitate your brain! Some people find it helpful to look at the picture below—which may also be on the wall of your TMS treatment space—depicting the activity in a depressed brain and the activity in the same, non-depressed brain. This is what TMS is working toward with you, to stimulate your brain enough so that it takes over and is "lit up" with generative activity! Some TMS participants choose to do the mental exercise of visualizing their own brains lighting up with neuronal firing as new growth happens during these weeks of TMS treatment, much like an athlete visualizes the plays they will make during the game so that they are ready and able.

Brain activity is reduced in depression[1]

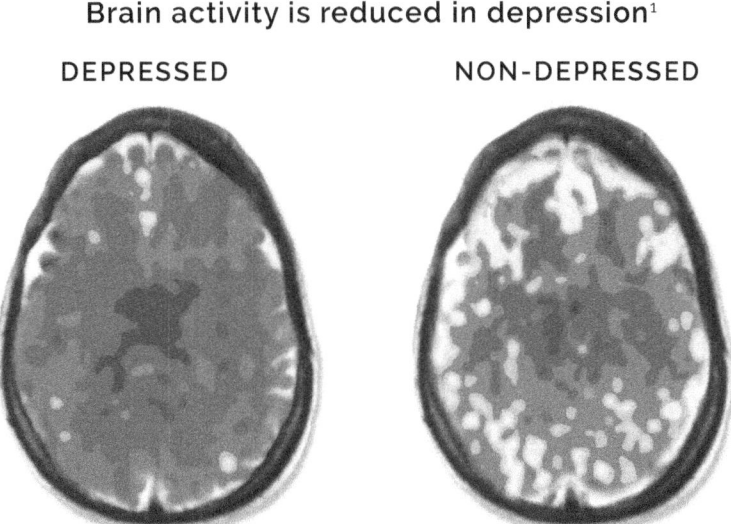

A PET scan measures vital functions such as blood flow, oxygen use, and blood sugar (glucose) metabolism.

Source: Mark George M.D. Biological Psychiatry Branch Division of Intramural Research Programs, NIMH 1993

You can keep yourself on your path to wellness during this important time by bringing attention back to the experience of something that is presently comfortable while you sit in the chair and by treating yourself with abundant kindness. Here are some examples of thoughts that you might introduce and cultivate in order to help you deal with fear, doubt or discomfort this week:

- I've shown up, that's important.
- This, too, shall pass.
- I am capable of keeping myself safe.
- Just take this breath.
- I will focus on my feet.

Turning Toward and Turning Away

Please notice what it's like when you admit what's really happening and believe it and bring kindness to yourself, compared to when you turn away from what's happening, and deny or belittle your feelings and berate yourself for reacting as you have to the experience. Is there a different thought you could introduce that might help? How about "It's not wrong that I am encountering any of this—thoughts, feelings, sensations—they make up my individual experience." The great mindful challenge is to be present and care for yourself within whatever *is*.

You Can Make Choices for Self-Care

You've likely noticed that in life there is so much you can't control. True. In the TMS treatment room, however, you are encouraged to control as much as you can to contribute to a more comfortable experience. As your treatment team has likely mentioned, you can usually dim the lights, play your music, watch whatever you want on the screen, sit quietly or chat, hold something or sit empty-handed. If there is anything you think of that might help make your treatment sessions better, just ask; your treatment team is there for you, and while it may not always be comfortable, there is often something you can do to improve your TMS treatment experience.

To further support themselves emotionally during the weeks of treatment, some participants also plan something that brings them joy and ease after each appointment or at the end of each week, rewarding themselves for the task they've accomplished. Perhaps you'd like to invite your support person to join you in this routine; celebration contributes positively to one's journey through difficulty toward a desired accomplishment.

The Mind

The Mindfulness Sidekick refers to "the mind" frequently, and you'll want to know exactly how it's used here. Dr. Daniel Siegel, a professor and interpersonal neurobiologist at UCLA, offers that

> "the mind can be thought of as the self-organizing, emergent process which is both embodied and relational, that regulates the flow of energy and information."[2]

In other words, the mind shares information across the brain, the body and the minds of other living beings. Inner experiences like thoughts, sensations and emotions are phenomena that arise in the mind, hidden from view, but that can be described once a person becomes aware that they are experiencing them. A person can best perceive these phenomena by slowing down, paying attention as they arise and acknowledging the arising as it occurs.

Inner experiences are something we often come to know from accidental training, by putting things together on our own. For example, when you felt sad as a child and an adult said, "Why are you so sad?" You could put together that the sensations you were having in your body meant you were experiencing something the people around you called "sad," which, you learned, somewhere along the line, was a feeling. Most children do not have the benefit of comprehensive Thought, Emotion and Sensation Training. By the way, we humans also experience visual images, memories, urges, and other inner experiences, but we'll just deal here with these big three and you can generalize from there.

Perhaps more people would understand and care for their minds better if they had been taught as children how to recognize inner experiences and care for themselves during their arising. Many adults fail to recognize that they are even having thoughts, or that feelings have arisen, or that their bodies are experiencing sensations, all of which might help guide them to actions for their own well-being. As a result, people often miss the experience all together or have difficulty understanding what's happening and how to be well in the swell of such experiences.

The Mind Is Like a Forest Full of Birds

Learning can lead to much better care. For example, if you go on a birdwatching expedition and you know nothing about birds, you might be able to spot a bird in a tree or one flying by, but you will not know the specifics of the bird, how it reproduces or makes its home, nor how it is interdependent with its environment and can be helped to flourish. You might enjoy the walk in the forest as you go birding, but you will certainly miss knowing what bird is calling, how the babies can survive in a storm, and which feathered friends need to be saved from extinction. You could also be at risk of being harmed or doing harm to a bird or to its habitat. On the other hand, once you become more specifically aware of the birds of your region, you might better appreciate their role in nature and you could be a contributor to helping the birds or the ecosystem.

Patience, non-striving, and beginner's mind—all attitudes of mindfulness— can be helpful as we both experience pleasures birding and also foster our own mental well-being. We are, in this case, learning about our inner experiences and how to strengthen those that carry us further along the path to our most desired life. Coincidentally, as birders, we would never try to scare a bird away; in fact, we'd quietly pause and stay to learn as much as we could about that bird so that nature could continue to function at its highest level. What would it mean if the woods were empty of birds? In a similar way, we can pause quietly to notice what's happening and learn to care for ourselves as whatever is flying around lands in us.

The relational part of the definition of the mind reminds us that we can communicate what we are thinking, feeling, or sensing to another person, and they can then connect with us in a way that either helps or hinders our best living. You'll read more about improving our communication with ourselves and others in Week Six when you learn about Compassionate Communication.

We'll Focus on the Big Three

While we might also choose to put visual images, urges, desires and more onto our list of inner experiences, *The Mindfulness Sidekick* will focus mainly on the three following aspects arising in your mind.

Feelings

In the 4th Century B.C., Aristotle referred to the feelings (or emotions) as being seated in the heart, but obviously, when we experience feelings, we are having sensations in the body and are understanding them through the cognitive processes in the brain. "You can name it to tame it," points to how labeling an emotion we perceive allows us to understand our experience and communicate it to others and also helps to calm our bodies' nervous systems, developing equanimity (mental calmness, evenness of temper, especially in a difficult situation.)[3] We can keep learning and building our vocabulary for emotions so that we are better able to distinguish among our experiences and are equipped to describe this experience to another so that they understand us better, which can lead to a sense of safety through being understood and believed.

> I **feel** . . . *afraid, joyful, anxious, hopeful, eager, proud, excited, tired, energetic, etc.* These are feelings.

> (Many more feeling words are available on the next page.)

Feelings that tend to arise when our needs are met

AFFECTIONATE
- compassionate
- open-hearted
- warm
- friendly
- sympathetic
- loving
- tender

ENGAGED
- absorbed
- engrossed
- fascinated
- involved
- alert
- enchanted
- interested
- spellbound
- curious
- entranced
- intrigued
- stimulated

HOPEFUL
- expectant
- encouraged
- optimistic

CONFIDENT
- empowered
- safe
- open
- secure
- proud

EXCITED
- amazed
- aroused
- eager
- giddy
- passionate
- animated
- astonished
- energetic
- invigorated
- surprised
- ardent
- dazzled
- enthusiastic
- lively
- vibrant

GRATEFUL
- appreciative
- touched
- moved
- thankful

INSPIRED
- amazed
- awed
- in wonder

JOYFUL
- amused
- happy
- tickled
- delighted
- jubilant
- glad
- pleased

EXHILARATED
- blissful
- enthralled
- rapturous
- ecstatic
- exuberant
- thrilled
- elated
- radiant

PEACEFUL
- calm
- centered
- fulfilled
- relaxed
- serene
- trusting
- clear headed
- content
- mellow
- relieved
- still
- comfortable
- equanimous
- quiet
- satisfied
- tranquil

REFRESHED
- enlivened
- rested
- rejuvenated
- restored
- renewed
- revived

This second list shows feelings that tend to arise when our needs are not met

AFRAID
- apprehensive
- frightened
- petrified
- terrified
- dread
- mistrustful
- scared
- wary
- foreboding
- panicked
- suspicious
- worried

ANNOYED
- aggravated
- displeased
- impatient
- dismayed
- exasperated
- irritated
- disgruntled
- frustrated
- irked

ANGRY
- enraged
- indignant
- outraged
- furious
- irate
- resentful
- incensed
- livid

AVERSION
- animosity
- disgusted
- horrified
- appalled
- dislike
- hostile
- contempt
- hate
- repulsed

CONFUSED
- ambivalent
- dazed
- mystified
- torn
- baffled
- hesitant
- perplexed
- bewildered
- lost
- puzzled

DISCONNECTED
- alienated
- bored
- distant
- numb
- withdrawn
- aloof
- cold
- distracted
- removed
- apathetic
- detached
- indifferent
- uninterested

DISQUIET
- agitated
- disconcerted
- rattled
- startled
- turbulent
- uneasy
- upset
- alarmed
- disturbed
- restless
- surprised
- in turmoil
- unnerved
- discombobulated
- perturbed
- shocked
- troubled
- uncomfortable
- unsettled

EMBARRASSED
- ashamed
- guilty
- chagrined
- mortified
- flustered
- self-conscious

FATIGUE
- beat
- exhausted
- sleepy
- worn out
- burnt out
- lethargic
- tired
- depleted
- listless
- weary

PAIN
- in agony
- devastated
- hurt
- regretful
- anguished
- grieving
- lonely
- remorseful
- bereaved
- heartbroken
- miserable

SAD
- depressed
- despondent
- disheartened
- heavy hearted
- unhappy
- dejected
- disappointed
- forlorn
- hopeless
- wretched
- despairing
- discouraged
- gloomy
- melancholy

TENSE
- anxious
- distraught
- frazzled
- nervous
- stressed out
- cranky
- edgy
- irritable
- overwhelmed
- distressed
- fidgety
- jittery
- restless

VULNERABLE
- fragile
- insecure
- sensitive
- guarded
- leery
- shaky
- helpless
- reserved

YEARNING
- envious
- nostalgic
- jealous
- pining
- longing
- wistful

© NonviolentCommunication.com

Thoughts

It is generally believed that we humans have more than 6000 thoughts a day! Thoughts are conceived of as electro-chemical reactions, signals that are transmitted from some of the 100 billion nerve cells called neurons, through the trillions of connections (called synapses) between neurons. On average, each connection transmits quickly—anywhere from one signal per second to 1,000 signals per second. While scientists know a bit about how thoughts are transported and why they do what they do, it is still very difficult to trace how a thought begins and how it arrives in our conscious mind. Scientists know that the prefrontal cortex has something to do with that, and reliable data suggests that mindfulness helps the prefrontal cortex calm the body down when thoughts agitate it, those very thoughts coming, somehow, from the same prefrontal cortex. Quite a complicated role this human brain plays, as both the problem and the solution!

> I **think**. . . *that TMS will work, that TMS will not work, that I will wait and see, that I can't handle this whole thing, that I can do what I need to this time, that I am being a wimp, that I am strong* . . . These are **thoughts**.

Often when we are not mindful, having a thought leads to being convinced of its truth. On the other hand, when we are mindful, we can take one step back and frame the experience as an observer of thinking, as in:

I am noticing that I am having the thought that . . ..

For example:

- *I am noticing that I am having the thought that* I am sick.
- *I am noticing that I am having the thought that* life is unfair.
- *I am noticing that I am having the thought that* I will never learn enough to feel all better.
- *I am noticing that I am having the thought that* I can never do everything this book wants me to do.

There might be some thoughts that feel good when they show up. For example:

- *I am noticing that I am having the thought that* I can change.
- *I am noticing that I am having the thought that* this might be interesting to learn something new.
- *I am noticing that I am having the thought that* I could finally be a meditator.

Yes, you are having lots of thoughts all the time and this is normal. When you can notice (and announce, if only to yourself) that you are "noticing that you are having a thought that," in that moment you also have an observing relationship with the thought—not more than that—and you can take action by turning your attention toward or away from that thought. In that moment, you are not stopping a thought, you are acting on moving your focus and refocusing on something else that is happening in this moment. When you take this tiny, awake action, you demonstrate that you are more vast than a small thought, no matter how powerful that thought has been in previous moments. The thought can then pass on through the vast space of awareness and you can notice what else is available to you, thus creating a new neural pathway leading to a new way of being!

Sensations

The Merriam Webster Dictionary defines sensations as:

a: immediate external stimulation of a sense organ often as distinguished from a conscious awareness of the sensory process

b: awareness (as of heat or pain) due to stimulation of a sense organ

c: a state of consciousness due to internal bodily changes: a sensation of hunger

d: an indefinite bodily feeling: a sensation of buoyancy[4]

>   I **sense**. . . *tightness in my chest, a lump in my throat, cold hands, shakiness, expansiveness, heaviness.* These are **sensations**.

When we train ourselves to bring attention to our body, we build our skill to balance the natural tendency to "live in our heads." Sensations describe our body awareness rather than our thoughts. When we pay attention to sensations, we live more from our bodies and we can center and ground into the direct experiences that come from the world we are in presently, rather than be carried away by the clouds of thoughts that come and go and that may be unrelated to the environment we are in.

An (Incomplete) List of Bodily Sensations to Help Describe Your Bodily Experience

- aglow
- moved
- tender

- cold
- shivery

- contracted
- disconnected
- frozen
- icy
- small

- burning
- crampy
- impulsive

- cozy
- oozy
- touched

- dark
- sweaty

- cut-off
- draining
- heavy
- imploding

- clenched
- hard
- knotted

- melting
- soft
- warm

- shaky
- trembling

- disappearing
- empty
- hiding
- invisible

- constricted
- hot
- red hot

It's All Just Information

It can be helpful to notice that any given feeling, thought or sensation might be comfortable, uncomfortable or neutral, and viewed nonjudgmentally, it's all just information. From a perspective of mindfulness practice, none of those common phenomena are wrong, they just happen and most often don't require analyzing, evaluating, fixing or being made to stop or disappear.

Feelings, thoughts, and sensations are all good information for this mindfulness adventure you are on. Just as if you are walking in the forest looking at the birds, or you are sitting on the beach watching waves, or you are at a museum seeing modern art, *being aware that you are watching is all you need to do.* You don't need to solve any of the moment-to-moment sensations, thoughts or feelings. And by observing and knowing that you are observing, you build awareness and you change your relationship to the difficult inner experiences that have caused trouble in the past. This takes a strong attitude of patience, trust, acceptance and curiosity. It takes intention of non-judging, non-striving, and of letting go. It takes generosity and gratitude, a kindness to yourself and a thankfulness for what you already have in your life moment-to-moment. And it takes watching closely and noticing that you are watching for some space to come between you and that thought, feeling or sensation. It's much easier to see the forest if a tree is not on top of you, and once you see the forest, you can see the spaces in between the trees. These spaces in between may be the moments of ease you experience, or a pause before you talk unkindly to yourself again. And little by little, TMS session after TMS session, deep breath after deep breath, you retrain your brain toward more awakeness and more kindness and toward actions that lead to more wellness and to your more valued life. Perhaps there are more moments worth noticing. Don't miss them, stay awake to what's happening!

Skills to Try

Skill One: Tuning In To What Is on Your Mindfulness Sidekick Playlist

This guided meditation will lead you through focusing on many aspects of your present experience, including what you see, hear, sense and feel. If at any point what you experience feels overwhelming, you can open your eyes and look around you, taking in information that affirms that you are safe. You can just rest there, with your eyes open, letting whatever you are experiencing be, and reminding yourself of your own resilience and capacity to be a support to yourself. When ready, you can tune back in to all of those internal experiences that are arising as you attend to the moment.

Skill Two: Breathing Meditation on Your Mindfulness Sidekick Playlist

The Breathing Meditation is a very basic yet powerful mindfulness practice. You will be guided through simply focusing on your breathing—paying attention to the flow of the breath and the way the body changes as you breathe. Using the breath as an anchor allows you to turn to breathing at any time if you start experiencing increased mindless and automatic thinking, undesired stress or unwanted emotions.

Home Practice

You can probably notice thoughts that show up again and again in your mind, like unwanted visitors who come often even though they are not invited and stay long enough so that they maybe should start paying rent! The more you listen to any one guided meditation, the more parts of it will show up naturally in your mind later and more helpfully. You do have some choice about which habituated thoughts play as you repeat and repeat things to yourself. You can replace the habituated "recordings" with something that calms your body and reassures you that you are OK, that you are safe, that you are good. Listen to the **Breathing Meditation** several times a day—it's not long—and you will start to notice that the process of mindful breathing becomes familiar, a new visitor you could actually live with! Remember, starting a new behavior is difficult and you might notice an urge to quit before change happens, with a thought like: "I am not good at meditating." That's just not workable. Being good at meditation means that you make time to do it, not that you have a blank and blissful mind for the period of sitting. Rather, making time to sit stillish and focusing on the breath *as best you can* is good meditation. As you bring an attitude of non-striving and patience to this meditation again and again, you'll feel the result of your practice. You might even catch yourself paying more attention to your breath throughout your day.

Writing Reflection

Right now—in this very moment—I am feeling: (insert feeling words here, not a thought!) (See pages 39–43 for two lists of feeling words.)

_____
_____
_____

Right now I am thinking:

_____
_____
_____

Right now I am sensing:

_____
_____
_____

During my breathing meditation practice, I have been noticing the following inner experiences (thoughts/feelings/sensations):

_____
_____
_____

This is how I am relating to the inner experiences coming up:

_____
_____
_____
_____

This is different from how I normally relate to thoughts/emotions/sensations because:

_____
_____
_____
_____

This change in the way I'm relating (however small) might lead me on a path to a more meaningful life because:

_____
_____
_____
_____

Nature Connection

Bring your attention to both the sky (seeing) and your breathing (sensing) Notice what's happening in the sky, what's passing through and what's staying there. If the sky is socked in with clouds, imagine the vast blue sky that is up above that relatively thin layer of clouds. Spend time, as you breathe, just noticing what you are experiencing and letting go. When you have finished, think about how clouds—like thoughts, feelings and sensations—change with the passage of time. Contemplate the idea that the only constant is change and that we can count on impermanence in everything.

Wise Words

Thoughts by Myra Viola Wilds (1915)

> What kind of thoughts now, do you carry
> In your travels day by day
> Are they bright and lofty visions,
> Or neglected, gone astray?
> Matters not how great in fancy,
> Or what deeds of skill you've wrought;
> Man, though high may be his station,
> Is no better than his thoughts.
> Catch your thoughts and hold them tightly,
> Let each one an honor be;
> Purge them, scourge them, burnish brightly,
> Then in love set each one free.

TMS Week Two

"Evolution has shaped our minds so that we are almost inevitably destined to suffer psychologically: to compare, evaluate and criticize ourselves; to focus on what we're lacking; to be dissatisfied with what we have; and to imagine all sorts of frightening scenarios, most of which will never happen. No wonder humans find it hard to be happy!"

—RUSS HARRIS

*"The bad news is time flies.
The good news is you are the pilot."*

—MICHAEL ALTSHULER

Accepting This Human Brain

Congratulations, you made it through what many people think is the most uncomfortable part of TMS treatment—the first handful of sessions. You may notice that you are tolerating the treatment slightly better this week. You may focus on discomfort at thoughts about whether what you did in the office during your sessions was OK with your TMS team. You've heard it before, but here it is again: you can take control in the TMS room to make your experience comfortable; you get to determine what works best for you each day. If you choose to distract yourself by chatting with your technician or by watching the screen, can you immerse yourself in noticing what you are seeing or hearing, bringing your full attention to that part of your present moment experience? This total permission to care for yourself in the chair, noticing what works for you and what doesn't is a mindfulness practice in itself. Your TMS provider will not be in each session, so your technician will be your steady daily companion, and you might experiment with asking for help when you need or want it.

It is certainly helpful and healthy to notice—and maybe even talk about—your mood as it changes throughout these days and weeks of TMS treatment. One day you might be in a cranky mood, another day exhausted, and another, quite serene. You will be able to write about those moods during your WRITING REFLECTION. (A longer list of feeling words is available in Week One.) Just like with most inner experiences, moods come and go much like weather patterns. You may like one mood more than others, but all of them are normal. The practice of mindfulness is the practice of releasing your expectation and your grip on the meaning of any mood and choosing to experience it but not beat yourself up for it. Loosening your grip might create the opportunity for your "mood weather" to shift toward something more to your liking. Remember, a mood doesn't mean any particular thing about you, so you might practice going easy on yourself and taking good care. As nun and meditation teacher Pema Chodron reminds, "You are the sky. Everything else—it's just the weather."

Understanding

This Brain, It's Only Human

That human brain of yours has evolved to see things as you've seen them before, to think thoughts that you've thought earlier and to experience life the way you've understood it previously. TMS helps by improving communication between the prefrontal cortex—which specializes in rational thinking—and the limbic system—which facilitates emotional experience and expression. TMS strengthens connections in the brain so that it both ignites helpful messages for calming down and extinguishes unhelpful messages more quickly and easily; this helps new learning to occur. Your effort to bring attention and the attitude of beginner's mind to your present moment will contribute to your brain's ability to heal itself from the oppressive patterning that marks the depression you've been under.

Of course, you will come upon obstacles to developing new neural pathways, and no treatment is a cure-all, but with the science-based influence of TMS and the continuous practice of generous acceptance through mindfulness, change can come and you can take small turns toward the experiences that lead to your own valued way of living. When you consciously choose to tune into what contributes to a rich, meaningful, purposeful life, you are aiding in expansion of the healthy neuropathways, leading yourself to increased awareness and improved ease toward healthy choices.

During any mindfulness practice, you will likely notice that the mind wanders away from the object of your attention and when you bring it back, it leaves again, just like a puppy that can slip through the puppy gate! This attentional escapism is normal human brain behavior and also a chance for you to foster patience, trust and nonjudgment. As you sit still in meditation for longer periods of time, you might be having any or all of the following thoughts in response to noticing how much your mind is wandering:

- I am bad at meditating.
- I can't do this, I can't seem to stay focused.

- I'd rather not try.
- Something is wrong with me, I'm worse than most people.
- This is stupid.

All of these thoughts are normal and reflect that you have a typical human brain! As you read in the previous chapter, the practice of noticing that your attention has wandered and waking up from that "trance of the wandering mind" and returning to the present moment sensations of breathing—if only for a brief second—*is* meditation. If you let go of expecting yourself to become like the storied monk in a mountain cave with a blank mind reaching nirvana, you'll have a chance to understand that this journey is all about tiny moments of letting go and embracing nonjudgment, not about perfection.

You Are a Sheep Herder

You might, instead of all those critical thoughts, like to think about your attention in this way. Imagine a sheep herder with a couple dozen ewes and lambs resting against a tree. The sheep might mostly stay together, making it relaxing for the herder, but every so often, a wandering sheep ambles away from the herd, causing the herder to get up and guide her back to the fold. The herder isn't angry because the herder knows that that sheep is not defective, that's just what sheep do—they wander. When the herder has brought the thought—oops, the sheep!—back to the grazing place, the shepherd sits down again to rest and digest. Good herders neither fear nor loathe the sheep and the very best sheep herders are those that love themselves and their ability to herd sheep without self-judgment. Your job description as a sheep herder with a healthy mind is to stay alert, but not alarmed. To keep your sheep from straying (and potentially getting eaten by a wolf) you'll need to be patiently watchful and curious, to do only what's necessary and to not worry too much about times when sheep will stray in the future. If you approach shepherding in this manner, you will find more calm and greener pastures!

Autopilot Makes The Brain's Work Easy, and Keeps You Reacting Mindlessly

Have you ever driven miles to someplace familiar and wondered how you got there, realizing you must not have paid attention along the way? These human brains operate best when we are firmly attentive as the pilot of our own life. We can bring full attention to a wonderful experience and be present to soak it up, and we can deal with a difficult challenge more easily when we bring our full attention to solving something or just coping. However, we spend much of our lives with a wandering mind and our brain, being the efficient machine that it is, allows this by letting our awake ("noticing you are noticing") part of our brain stay "offline." This autopilot mode literally saves calories for our body to keep on going without threat of overspending our calories and running on empty. When we are on autopilot in this way, our brains follow directions on a flight path we've already been on before and we tend to react—rather than respond mindfully—to whatever life brings us. This automatic pilot experience might conserve brain energy, but it also causes us to miss out on the newness of each moment, make appropriate choices in a given situation, and forfeit the chance to change long-held patterned behaviors that don't serve us on our path to a rich, purposeful life.

Here are some examples of reacting on autopilot instead of responding mindfully:

- Tuning out the the fear in your child's voice when they ask if they have to go to school and snapping, "Yes, you do, because I said so," instead of investigating what's going on that's making your child want to stay home;
- Eating dessert after each dinner because that's what you always do, even when you are full, instead of making a conscious decision after each dinner, depending on what's best for your body that evening;
- Deciding not to take a walk because it's raining outside when you have known it's best to get daily movement into your life, instead of thinking how good it will feel if you get outside and get movement, even if you are a bit wet.

While all of the above first reactions take less energy because you are not awake and focused on the present situation, you (on autopilot) are likely to miss waking up and taking an action that is more aligned with your values and that directs you to your desired life.

Helping a Brain on Depression <u>and</u> on Autopilot

Depression can cause a person to have a preponderance of thoughts about not being good enough or not being capable. This repetition of difficult thoughts can slip us into automatic pilot, a sort of trance, as a way to minimize the pain of such self-loathing thoughts. When we find ways to be self-supportive, we can pay attention, awaken, let go of judgment, and in doing so, focus on the positive that empowers us to do more self-supportive actions. Here are some questions you might ask yourself to wake you from the trance of the self-disrespecting autopilot:

- *What is right about you?*
- *What have you done well?*
- *How have things gone well for you/how have you been lucky lately?*
- *How have you made the world a better place lately?*

You can always apply what you are learning about mindfulness to your TMS experience:

- What are the pleasant parts about coming to treatment each day?
- What tiny bits of progess have you seen in your own commitment to TMS or in results of your treatment?
- How is today's emotional state different from one last week?

Yoga: Awaken to the Body

This week, you'll also be introduced to a gentle yoga practice in order to invite awareness into the body, to further wake you up to what's happening within you. When you are tuned in to what's actually happening, you can explore the sensations in the body and revel in how the breath and the body are working together. Painful sensations can be noticed and understood as helpful information to guide your body's own movements and subsequent behaviors. When we use the best and latest information about what is happening in our bodies, we can move better and tend to our bodies, limiting injury and maximizing being present. Using the attitudes of generosity and gratitude, we might even celebrate what our body is able to do! And of course, there are so many good yoga classes online and likely in your community. It's easy to access yoga that will support your well-being.

Take Yourself Back to Your Values

You might notice also this week that learning to spend more time in formal mindfulness practice can bring uncomfortable thoughts, feelings and sensations that challenge your motivation and mood. If you are experiencing a muddled sense of why you are doing this work, or having a dip in your motivation, perhaps you can notice that experience without much judgment and with a bit of patient acceptance. Rereading your original reasons for participating in TMS and mindfulness (WRITING REFLECTION, in the Week Zero) might increase your motivation to do the work necessary to change that human brain of yours.

Be With It Rather Than React To It

Remember, you are learning to *be with*, rather than to *react to* what's happening in the present moment. Noticing in the moment that you are on autopilot and waking up to choose your actions helps you to notice and disengage from the thoughts, feelings and sensations that arise without our bidding and ultimately fosters a less difficult relationship with those inner experiences.

Where you might typically struggle to fix or to escape from difficult inner experiences in a given situation, mindful noticing allows you to drop the struggle, notice what's happening, embrace nonjudgment and stay connected with your values. You are then well-positioned to act from choice instead of react from habit. This being awake can lead you further on the path to your chosen life.

Skill to Try

Standing Yoga on your Mindfulness Sidekick Playlist

This guided yoga session is a good way to turn off autopilot and be more fully present. In standing yoga, you will be invited to turn your attention to your body and all the marvelous bending, folding, straightening and balancing your body can do. Stay with the body and the sensations that arise as you move and let go of judgment. Of course, your attention will wander many, many times while you practice yoga. Can you catch the moments when you notice that wandering mind and can you gently bring yourself back to you there, on the yoga mat? The breath can play a role as an object of focus during yoga. As you get comfortable doing the simple moves in these videos, you may find that you want to pause the video here and there to practice just being in the body. This is an example of the mindful attitude of non-striving, bringing attention to the body just for the sake of noticing you are alive in it.

The more yoga you do, the easier it will be and the more your body will become accustomed to the moves and poses. Whether an expert or a first timer on a yoga mat, let beginner's mind influence you as you notice and let pass thoughts about how yoga *should be* and allow yourself to experience how yoga *is* today. Sometimes we rob ourselves of pleasure because our minds are focused on striving for something or thinking about the future. Let yoga be a time of non-striving and of just being in the body as best you can.

Here are some examples of questions that you might ask yourself this week as you practice yoga:

- How do I experience my feet meeting with the mat?
- What region of my body is pain-free?
- How am I experiencing my ability to balance myself upright, despite years of difficulty and the power of gravity?
- As I let go of each breath, what is the experience of release specifically doing in my body?
- Where do I feel strong in my body?

Home Practice

Begin to notice when you are noticing in your walking around life. Start by choosing one daily activity that you pay attention to, like brushing your teeth, starting your car or coming and going through your front door. Notice your thoughts, sensations and feelings in this moment and release judgment *as best you can*.

Practice Breathing Meditation or Standing Yoga each day. Remember that the idea is not "Can I do it right, yes or no?" but rather, "Hmmmm. . .What am I noticing I am doing, thinking, feeling, sensing, and how am I relating to it all?"

Pay attention to how you are talking to yourself, thinking about yourself, and relating to this experience. Would you encourage loved ones to talk to themselves like you talk to yourself? Is there some better way to do this? And then, when you don't do this "better way" perfectly, can you practice trust and nonjudgment and keep on trying anyway?

You might have to encourage—even force—yourself to practice mindfulness, through thoughts of not wanting to, a sensation of heaviness in the body, feelings of dread or thoughts of dislike. What a great opportunity to notice what is happening and to be light with yourself. This "not wanting to" experience is just a passing cloud, not necessarily information that must be acted upon, especially if it doesn't lead to behaviors that you value on the way to your most meaningful life.

Writing Reflection

I am noticing that, in general, I have the following moods or feeling states during these days:

___

___

___

I also am noticing that I am relating to these moods or feelings states with/by:

___

___

___

During the yoga practice, I am noticing:

___

___

___

What is different from how I normally relate is:

___

___

___

___

Yoga might help me stay on my chosen path by:
_____
_____
_____

Yoga might contribute to my more purposeful life because:
_____
_____
_____

In general, I am noticing that I:
_____
_____
_____
_____

In general, I am noticing that I am having difficulty with:
_____
_____
_____
_____

When I get stuck, I am working with my struggle by:

_____
_____
_____
_____

I am noticing being on automatic pilot when:

_____
_____
_____
_____

I am noticing turning off automatic pilot by:

_____
_____
_____
_____

Since I started TMS, one thing that I value doing is:

_____
_____
_____
_____

Nature Connection

Find a tree that you see frequently. Stand still and spend five minutes or so examining every single aspect of the tree's physical characteristics. As you observe, tune in also to you standing there in front of it, rooted in place just like the tree. Tune into the ways in which your body feels tree-like, from your feet to the top of your head. Staying rooted, you can move and pause, move and pause and then notice what you have in common with the tree again. To end this session, talk to the tree about what it does for humans like you, and express your gratitude. Then talk to your own body about what it does for *you* and offer gratitude. Throughout the week, you can revisit the same tree or examine new trees and connect with them and your own body in the same way.

Wise Words

The Guest House by Jalaluddin Rumi, translated and permission given by Coleman Barks

This being human is a guest house.
Every morning a new arrival.
A joy, a depression, a meanness,
some momentary awareness comes
as an unexpected visitor.
Welcome and entertain them all!
Even if they're a crowd of sorrows,
who violently sweep your house
empty of its furniture,
still, treat each guest honorably.
He may be clearing you out
for some new delight.
The dark thought, the shame, the malice,
meet them at the door laughing,
and invite them in.
Be grateful for whoever comes,
because each has been sent
as a guide from beyond.

TMS Week Three

"Between stimulus and response there is a space. In that space is our power to choose our response. In our response lies our growth and our freedom."

—VIKTOR FRANKL

"Turning to the body can be a radical act."

—AMY HALLORAN-STEINER

Knowing the Mind and Being in the Body

You have likely finished about ten TMS treatments—well done! Now that you know generally what to expect with the TMS treatment itself, you might notice that your self-care while sitting in the TMS chair has improved. You may notice feeling a bit more confident with tolerating the treatment, and less fearful about coming to the sessions. Some people even notice taking pleasure in the thought that each short session is time for them to pause and remind themselves that they are doing something for their best care. If you are recognizing that the choice to do these sessions is right for you, then you might notice tension easing in the shoulders, or a lightening of that sense of weightedness on your body in general. Or . . . you might notice that you have the thought that you dislike showing up, that you'd prefer to be at work—or anywhere, really! Or . . . you might notice feelings of panic or disappointment and the sensation of a clenching in your throat or cramping in your stomach, all of which you likely want to turn away from. Or . . . you might notice yourself patiently waiting for change to happen, shut off to any feelings or sensations; and you might have the thought that you will wait until (insert future date here) before you make any judgment about whether this was a good idea. Or . . . Perhaps you are noticing very few thoughts, feelings and sensations.

It's OK to notice what your experience actually is these days and to bring an attitude of nonjudgment to your experience, letting go of your expectations about how you thought you'd be. There is a wide variety of responses during Week Three. Your motivation might rise or sink. You might notice no shift in mood, or some changing of the mood tides. If the outcome is not yet what you expected, you might have thoughts that quitting is the best thing, that something is wrong, or that you won't feel better, ever.

If you have become aware of your thoughts and feelings and have let go of judgment even just a little, then you have tasted mindful awareness. And while mindful awareness may not be the bliss you've wanted—may even be slightly painful—what you are noticing is real, and you are capable of noticing thoughts, emotions and sensations and of creating the bit of space that comes when you can notice those phenomena as passing experiences.

Remember, every participant responds differently to TMS. Rather than developing expectations for your experience, you can use beginner's mind to prevent the suffering of disappointment about life not meeting your expectations and create a smoother path forward to the life that is best suited for you.

Understanding

How Thoughts Become Automatic and How To Free Yourself From Them

Neurons connected by dendrites make up neural pathways that are created in the brain based on our habits and behaviors, such as having a thought or eating sugar when sad. The number of dendrites increases when a behavior is performed more frequently. Many people talk about these neural pathways being grooved into our brains, deeper and deeper with each repeated behavior.

When brain cells communicate frequently with one another, the connection between them strengthens and the messages get passed more quickly and easily on this same pathway. The thought we frequently tell ourselves, or the action of reaching for the sugary food we want becomes automatic. Driving, riding a bike, even simple math calculations are examples of (positive) complicated behaviors that we do automatically because neural pathways have formed. When a person wants to change a behavior, they can bring attention to the new, desired action to train their brain to create new neural pathways, which get stronger and stronger with repetition, and soon the desired thought or behavior becomes their automatic and normal behavior.

It might be interesting to notice your pattern of thinking lately, especially how your mind is judging TMS and your own performance in treatment. You might have had some of these thoughts pass through your mind this week about TMS:

- Things will turn out well. / Things are not going to turn out well.
- I can do this. / I can't do this.
- I am capable of changing. / I am not capable of changing.
- This is what I wanted. / This is not what I wanted.
- I am a success. / I am a failure.
- This is worth it. / This is not worth it.

It's valuable to notice that you are having these thoughts so that you can make some space between the thought and your belief about you. There are many ways to notice you are having a thought and to create that space for the thought to just pass through so it doesn't "get stuck." You can:

- imagine the thoughts are written on leaves, floating down a stream right past where you are sitting. No point in getting up and chasing after them;
- visualize the thoughts as train cars on a train that you are seeing in the distance as you sit up high on a hill. While you know the train is there, you are not riding it, so it doesn't take you anywhere;
- be like the vast blue sky, doing nothing as the thoughts (clouds of all shapes, sizes and tones of white and grey) pass through you. No matter how many thoughts pass through you, you are not impacted by the content of these thoughts;
- ponder that these thoughts are not THE TRUTH but rather just some pages of a script that your brain started reading and memorized for other situations too, even when the situation doesn't match the lines in the script.

Noticing More Experiences and Naming Them

During Week Three you might also notice that you are becoming more aware of the feelings that are arising. TMS treatment stimulates emotional centers of the brain - strengthening connection to this area with the more rational thinking parts of your brain. When you notice them, can you put words to them? The maxim "You can name it to tame it," can remind you that bringing any feeling into present moment awareness without judging or acting on it can help that feeling's intensity diminish, so that you can recognize it as just information to help you learn about yourself and what you need. When you meet your needs, you can move further on the path to your most cherished life.

In Week Three you might also notice more frequently what you are doing because of what thoughts and feelings are arising. Remember that when you are not on autopilot and are awake to the present moment, you can have the presence of mind to choose to pause. Pausing gives you an opening to behave in a way that aligns with your values and turns you toward solutions. If you embody being vast like the sky, then doing nothing can be the best thing you can do until those pesky clouds pass through.

Have You Thought About Counseling?

Sometimes we need a person outside of our family and friend group to remind us of our values and to teach us improved ways of living and coping. Perhaps you already have a relationship with a mental health professional to help you sort through the varied challenges in your life. If not, you might consider finding a counselor to meet with regularly. One study found that adding therapy to TMS increased depression remission (meaning little to no depression remaining) rates by 16%.[1] We humans evolved as intensely social animals and we need trusted others to help us learn about ourselves. Well-trained mental health practitioners can reflect our best possibilities and encourage us to persist in forming the life we want, holding us accountable for the behavior change that will support that life. When you choose a therapist or a counselor, it's important to feel a connection and to see that they are accurate listeners and observers, and that they act in appropriate and ethical ways. If you feel that something is off, or that they don't make an effort to really understand you, it's a good idea to talk to them about your concerns or to find someone else to work with. A good practitioner is like a guide hired to help you hike your way through mountainous terrain. A counselor is knowledgeable regarding the landscape of the mind and can encourage and support you as you make the often difficult and tiring sojourn forward on the path to your most meaningful life. (For info on finding a therapist, see Week Three, Note #2.)

Get to Know What The Mind Is

This week, it might be helpful to reflect upon how the brain and body are interconnected. Whether you ponder this with a therapist or on your own, it's good to know what you are pondering. The mind is defined here (thanks again to Dr. Dan Siegel) as the emergent, self-organizing, embodied, and relational process that regulates the flow of energy and information. The mind arises from a system of energy and information flow within the body, the brain and among other living beings. We can take into account the interplay between: the sense organs and the brain that processes the information; the limbic and adrenal systems that regulate, mitigate and communicate priorities for safety and survival to the body from the brain and back again; and the relational dynamics between a person and the emergent processes (minds) of the other living things the person comes in contact with.

With your intention to remain present and curious moment-to-moment, you can learn to work wisely with your thoughts, your emotions and your body sensations even as you experience stress, and to note how the stress shows you the above connection. Acceptance of, and gratitude for these natural patterns-of-mind help us to bring attitudes of curiosity and beginner's mind to noticing and learning from the habituated patterns that your brain has developed and cemented as time has gone by. While it appears that our habituated behaviors are unchangeable ("you can't teach an old dog new tricks" sort of thing) contemporary science of the mind shows us that your brain can learn new patterns and can grow and change for the duration of your life. All humans undergo conditioned patterning of the mind, reflected in the sayings, "what you know you grow" and "cells that fire together wire together." Choosing the habit of mindfulness can set helpful patterns of behavior into the brain that then contribute to a life lived more awake and in line with one's values.

Is What You Are Doing Helping?

Learning mindfulness with TMS gives you the opportunity to take yourself off automatic pilot and to wake up to what's happening in the moment, staying aware enough to clearly discern whether what is happening is contributing to your wellness or not. For example:

- Is sitting there on your couch (instead of going to the water exercise class you planned on) getting you further on your path to a healthy, purposeful life? What would be a better way to spend your next hour?
- Does texting an argument with your sister (instead of taking a pause and reminding yourself that you want a better relationship with her) contribute to your best self? What could you do or not do just then to follow your desired path?
- If you purchase the couple of bottles of wine you are considering, what sensations will you have the morning after you drink three glasses? What feelings will you likely have at the end of the week after you've drunk all that wine? What might you choose to do instead that takes you further toward your best self?

To accurately anticipate the answers to these questions, you'll need to be awake enough to access your thoughts, feelings and sensations and to evaluate the consequences of your potential behaviors. It helps to have a trusted mental health practitioner who will communicate honestly and might urge your continued effort not to avoid what is happening and to behave in ways that support your most meaningful life.

Being In The Body

Using mindfulness to notice our own habituated brain patterns often leads us to the body and the many sensations that are happening there at any given moment. As your ability to notice body sensations improves, you will be able to tune in more deeply to what's happening without fear or control. Instead of turning away from unpleasant sensations, you can turn your attention toward them and just notice they are happening. You can treat the body with an attitude of patience and trust, because the body remembers the past, and the information the body gives us in the present helps us understand ourselves more for the future. Eventually, mindful awareness of sensations can help you abide most bodily sensations and respond to what the body truly needs. Your awareness can be vast—much, much bigger than the distinct sensations you notice passing through the body at any one time.

Overwhelm Happens

During any intense internal or external experience, including in the body scan you'll learn to practice this week, a person can feel overwhelmed by the sensations they experience. Remember the idea of a gentle walk in the woods, with a chance to easily notice the birds flitting around you? Overwhelm might be more like a huge group of ravens (called, interestingly, an *unkindness*) who swoop in and not only grab your attention but make you feel unsafe, wanting to flee this birdwatching-turned-avian attack scenario. This reactive desire to flee the overwhelm felt in the body is normal, but not something you have to endure; you can open your eyes and find yourself there in the place your body is. You can turn your head to see completely around you, notice your position in the space and take in where you are in relation to others. You can take deep breaths, elongating the outbreath to ground and calm you. You have the choice to tune into your safety.

Bring Curiousity, Notice What You Can, Introduce a Helpful Thought

Either in your walking around life, or in a formal body scan meditation, if you experience intense sensation in your body without accompanying overwhelming disorientation or fear and would like to work with the sensation, you might consider bringing curiosity along with the breath to this area. You may notice that your thoughts are judging:

- *"This pain is so bad, it's like I could be dying"* or
- *"I am really messed up if I am sensing this, something is really wrong with me"* or
- *"I'll never be free of this discomfort"* or
- *"See, I really can't do this because. . ."* or even
- *"I love this sensation! I should do this all the time so I can feel this more!"* or
- *"This means I'm getting better, so that's good, so that means. . ."* or
- *"I bet this is the only time I'll ever feel this way, it probably won't happen again."*

You may notice you are having feelings: fear, upset, sadness, frustration, disappointment, or joy, eagerness, hope, excitement, ecstasy, yearning.

You can introduce a thought like:

- *"Nothing terrible is happening. I am just having sensations and resulting thoughts and feelings"* or
- *"I am safe and just paying attention, practicing a healthy habit"* or
- *"These are simply sensations, thoughts and feelings"* or
- *"I am much more vast than any (single or cluster of) sensations, thoughts and feelings"* or
- *"This is a good feeling and I can appreciate it while I have it, but don't need to hold on to it."*

And when you are ready to turn toward the sensations again, do so with awakened care and gentleness. You can also imagine that you are breathing in whatever you need (courage, safety, connection, love, letting go) and breathing out toward the intense sensation, softening and releasing with each exhalation.

You can notice any of this phenomena as you'd notice a cloud moving through the sky: the cloud changes shape or stays more or less the same. It momentarily obscures the sun. It is moving at some velocity. It is not of your creation. It doesn't predict much at all.

Fleeing in the Mind Makes Sense but Doesn't Help Long-Term

In your everyday life, without awareness, on autopilot, you aren't able to pause and decide what action to take to care for yourself during a strong sensation. You might:

- ignore it
- get frustrated at it
- block it
- get angry at yourself or others
- hurry through what you are doing
- put yourself down
- minimize the effect of it
- do something to just go away (like spacing out, Facebook, shopping, alcohol, drugs, gambling)

These are all effective escape techniques, but they can keep you up at night, ruin your peacefulness, health or relationships. A body scan—and paying attention to sensations generally—helps you tune in and take care of yourself in a potentially better way than escaping what is happening. If the sensation you are experiencing feels too intense and you won't be able to focus at all if it doesn't go away, you can always pay more attention to what is outside of you, such as counting all the square things you see or all the blue things you find and then returning when you can to that experience which is passing through you.

Emotions Are Waves You Can Surf

Finally, intense sensation can bring with it intense emotion. These are just temporary clouds passing, or maybe you'd like to conceive of these emotions as waves on the sea of your experience. You might simply acknowledge the waves are coming because you know that you can't stop a wave on the ocean, but you can surf it. In the case of emotion, you can do the same, perhaps with a surfboard of trust and non-striving, breathing through the most difficult parts. No matter the challenge, can you treat yourself with loving-kindness and generosity, knowing that you are acting with courage by even showing up?

In addition to *taming* what you are sensing, *naming* sensations also allows you to befriend them. (A list of sensation words can be found on page 47; feel free to add to that list.)

Skills to Try

Skill One: Body Scan on your Mindfulness Sidekick Playlist

The Body Scan is a gentle activity that continues the theme of *present moment focus* by expanding your practice of paying attention to the body. Following the guidance, you'll systematically move attention from one area of the body to the next until you've invited awareness to all areas of the body. The Body Scan is practiced lying down in a comfortable enough position, but perhaps not *so* comfortable that you will fall asleep. If you fall asleep easily, then perhaps you can do this Body Scan sitting up or with one arm propped up while lying down so that it wakes you when you fall asleep. Whatever the case, if sleepiness becomes one of your experiences during this activity, then that might be helpful information for you! The point of the Body Scan is to turn toward each experience in your body. The natural result of being more present in your body is that you are paying less attention to your thoughts and making more space for what is actually happening in the present moment in your body.

Skill Two: Every Little Victory on your Mindfulness Sidekick Playlist

This guided meditation will lead you through a series of openings for you to notice what victories and positive experiences you have had and are having. You will be invited to turn to the body to get curious about and accept the physical experiences taking place as a result of your private investigation.

Home Practice

During the week, invite awareness to any sensations that arise in the body. Do not try to dampen the sensations, just notice them. Pay attention to what your "escape" behaviors are and notice when you are successful in turning toward the experience. This practice of mindfulness during your regular day is an example of an *informal* mindfulness practice and can take as little as 15 seconds and as much as you allow.

Bring awareness to moments of reactivity, exploring them and using the breath to slow things down before responding. If you miss that chance, then notice being caught in a reactive moment and try—even though you are in the middle of difficulty—to offer a mindful response.

Practice any of your new mindfulness tools: Body Scan, Standing Yoga, or Mindful Eating, doing one each day and mixing them through the week.

Writing Reflection

During the body scan, I noticed:
___
___
___

I am noticing that when I have uncomfortable sensations in my body, I try to avoid them by:
___
___
___

To help create a sense of safety, I can notice the following comfortable sensations in my body:
___
___
___

This way of noticing and turning toward my sensations is different because:
___
___
___

This way of noticing might contribute to my general wellness and to progression along the path to my best life by:

_____
_____
_____

I brought my attention back to the present moment experience of my body by:

_____
_____
_____

Bringing my attention back to the present experience in my body will help me/not help me because:

_____
_____
_____

Here are times I paused this week. . . . and the outcome of each time I chose to pause is:

_____
_____
_____
_____

Despite setbacks, challenges and discomfort, I choose to continue with TMS treatment, because:

_____
_____
_____

I want to do some things differently in my life, including:

_____
_____
_____
_____

If I really invest, I imagine my life will be different because:

_____
_____
_____
_____

I am already learning:

_____
_____
_____
_____

I already see changes happening in me, including:

_____
_____
_____
_____

I am struggling with:

_____
_____
_____
_____

I am encouraged by:

_____
_____
_____
_____

My body can allow me to:

_____
_____
_____
_____

Nature Connection

Do a body scan outside, either lying down or sitting on the earth, even if it's really cold, maybe wrap yourself in blankets and try a short Body Scan session, coming inside to finish it if you can no longer withstand the cold. Notice in the same manner you noticed before, only this time pay special attention to your skin, your temperature and the other ways your body interacts with nature.

Wise Words

"Pausing is an opportunity to clearly see the wants and fears that are driving us. During the moments of a pause, we become conscious of how the feeling that something is missing or wrong keeps us leaning into the future, on our way somewhere else. This gives us a fundamental choice in how we respond: We can continue our futile attempts at managing our experience, or we can meet our vulnerability with . . .wisdom."

—Tara Brach

Two Wolves - A Cherokee Parable

An old Cherokee chief was teaching his grandson about life. . .

"A fight is going on inside me," he said to the boy, "It is a terrible fight and it is between two wolves. One is evil - he is anger, envy, sorrow, regret, greed, arrogance, self-pity, guilt, resentment, inferiority, lies, false pride, superiority, self-doubt, and ego. The other is good - he is joy, peace, love, hope, serenity, humility, kindness, benevolence, empathy, generosity, truth, compassion, and faith. This same fight is going on inside you - and inside every other person, too."

The grandson thought about it for a minute and then asked his grandfather, "Which wolf will win?"

The old chief simply replied, "The one you feed."

TMS Week Four

"Gratitude unlocks the fullness of life. It turns what we have into enough, and more. It turns problems into gifts, failures into successes, the unexpected into perfect timing, mistakes into important events. . .and disconnected situations into important and beneficial lessons. Gratitude makes sense of our past, brings peace for today, and creates a vision for tomorrow."

—MELODY BEATTIE

Summoning Gratitude

Conventional wisdom says it takes 21 days to make a habit, so let's call TMS a habit that is leading to better mental health. Maintaining your commitment up to Week Four is a victory and an important marker along your path to your most meaningful life. It's important to celebrate even the tiniest victories, and getting to Week Four is more robust than tiny; you have completed about a third of your TMS treatment! Friendly praise and encouragement are an important snack to pull out on this long and sometimes arduous journey to mental wellness. This practice of noticing with joy and letting yourself feel it is called "growing the good," something teacher and psychologist Rick Hanson encourages us to do for our mental wellness.[1]

This week, you may be noticing subtle changes in your mood; you might be more interested in doing activities, taking better care of your physical self, making more plans to socialize and sticking with them. Perhaps you can perceive a new sensation of lightness in the body or hear yourself say something that surprises you. Perhaps a person close to you is also noticing changes, hearing a new tone in your voice, or seeing a light in your eyes. Be sure to share your own subtle observations and feedback you've received with your treatment team. Or . . . you may be experiencing a dip back into depression this week and may be able to notice you are having the thought that this TMS stuff isn't going to work. You might notice this dip resolving within this week. Or . . . you might not have noticed much of a change at all over the first three weeks and be having the thought that your depressed emotional state has not let up and that something must be wrong, perhaps even that something is wrong with you.

If you are having any very difficult thoughts about your treatment, please mention them to your TMS provider so that they can consider an adjustment to your treatment. Notice the judgments and accompanying feelings and sensations when you can, and remember that change takes time. In fact, scientific wisdom disagrees with conventional wisdom and points to some average period more like 66 days to make a habit,[2] so keep on going, no matter the private experiences you are struggling with. Perhaps taking deep breaths and catching the judgment in the light of your attention will help you examine what's happening, then bring an attitude of patient acceptance and letting go of whatever expectation you are holding on to. Some examples of this holding that might be causing you trouble are:

- *thinking you should be feeling something in particular and you are not;*
- *feeling upset with yourself or someone else because treatment (or something else you wanted in life) is not going according to plan;*
- *feeling disappointed by someone you love who has let you down or failed to see you for who you believe yourself to be.*

When releasing a routine breath, perhaps you can soften the body, staying awake to what's happening there in the present moment and using the attitudes of patience and gratitude to see yourself through this particular unpleasant weather pattern.

Thoughts such as "I knew it wouldn't work," or "I figured I'd be the one person not to respond to TMS" are normal if you aren't seeing improvement. Feelings of hopelessness and fear also make sense. Even though it's great to be halfway along in treatment, it still means there is half of TMS treatment left to transform your brain, so perhaps you can employ optimism instead of falling prey to negative thinking that "TMS won't work." You might assess how long it took your brain to create the thought patterns it has created—a lifetime—so a few weeks might be considered a relatively small amount of time.

Jennifer Behnke, PMHNP, a pioneering TMS practitioner in Oregon, tells the story of a TMS participant who noticed no improvement at all during treatment and then his depression went away after treatment was completely over![3] Remember that your brain has an amazing capacity to change and grow. With every TMS treatment, your brain cells are learning more effective ways to communicate with each other in support of your well-being. As with most anything, practices such as TMS and mindfulness take time to change the brain but lead to long-term transformation once the patterns are established.

The TMS treatment journey and, indeed, the ups and downs of a typical human life mimic the high and low waves in the ocean tides. Your growing capacity to stay awake and provide self-compassion lets you surf on top of the waves. Of course, once in a while a wave might topple you, and you can use trust and acceptance to relax your body and remind yourself that you are OK. In the words of Joseph Campbell, "Let the world be as it is and learn to rock with the waves."

Understanding

Let Us Be Steeped in Gratitude

Gratitude is an action that affirms goodness that is present. In honing our gratefulness, we can acknowledge and celebrate that there are good people, things, events and infuences in the world, and can point to positivity we have received. While life is not all good, there are many, many beneficial aspects in life. Gratitude doesn't preclude negativity, but it allows us to recognize and put a name to the good.

When we pinpoint the good, we can also give airtime to the source of the goodness. With humility, we can recognize that most goodness starts from somewhere outside of ourselves, and with humility, we can also recognize our vital dependence on others. We can acknowledge that so many other people, systems and even higher powers (if you have a spiritual orientation) provide the many big and small contributions to the blessings in our lives. We can create a regular habit of bringing attention to aspects of our lives for which we are grateful, which can lead to improved psychological well-being. Some studies have found that gratitude practices—like writing a gratitude letter—can increase people's happiness and overall positive mood.[4] Studies have found that people who participated in a regular activity of accounting for things for which they were grateful improved their life satisfaction and sense of self-worth,[5] alleviated symptoms of depression and boosted positive affect,[6] increased optimism and happiness,[7] and decreased body dissatisfaction in women.[8]

Here are some prompts to get your gratitude juices flowing:

- I'm grateful for these three family members:
- I'm grateful for these three friends:
- I'm grateful for these three inventions:
- I'm grateful for these three non-human living beings:
- I'm grateful for these three teachers from my youth:
- I'm grateful for these three things at home:
- I'm grateful for these three people who cared about me when I was young:
- I'm grateful for this month every year:
- I'm grateful for these three places on earth:
- I'm grateful for three things I hear right now:
- I'm grateful for three things I see right now:
- I'm grateful for three things I smell regularly:
- I'm grateful for three things I touch/feel regularly:
- I'm grateful for these three things I taste regularly:

And here are several other gratitude activities that are commonly accepted as gratitude boosters:

- A gratitude journal for periodic reflecting on good things in life;
- A letter to someone you feel grateful for, detailing why;
- A jar that you put money in when you think of good things about your day and then pass the money on to someone who could use it;
- A list of gratitudes added to each time you notice yourself complaining about something.

You can certainly make up your own activity to boost a practice of gratitude and see if it helps you focus more on the good things in the present and less on the difficult things. You be the judge and maybe you will judge less and smile more.

Skills to Try

Skill One: Sitting Meditation on your Mindfulness Sidekick Playlist

This Sitting Meditation practice is a longer meditation exercise than the earlier Breathing Meditation. In this Sitting Meditation practice, you'll use many of your senses and bring attention to your breath, your thoughts and the source of your thoughts, as you practice opening to body sensations and making safe space for them when they get intense. You will be led to practice "choiceless awareness," which notices everything at once as it arrives and falls away, one moment at a time. Please be patient with yourself. Perhaps just staying with the breath is enough for now. The benefits of mindfulness can be attained with very simple practices, so there is no need to do more complicated practices if simple ones achieve an easeful presence that supports movement toward your chosen life.

Skill Two: Grateful for Each Little Victory on your Mindfulness Sidekick Playlist

Bring special attention to anything you notice that is different and better during this week. Grow the good by really paying attention to details of what's particularly good about that experience or how that good experience happened. Sink into all the possible gratitude in this little (or big) victory.

Some examples:

- *I tasted a cookie fresh out of the oven. The taste was sweet and delicious, and it also felt so warm and soft and chewy, which they weren't once they cooled. I felt lucky to have gotten one right out of the oven.*
- *I sat at the table and listened to my father, really listened, for the first time in a while. Even though I've been so frustrated with him lately, I had the thought that we don't have much time left together and I resolved to make the best of it, even if he is angry and grumpy a lot of the time. I felt grateful for our relationship.*

- *I finished all my errands today. My library books were returned before the deadline and I was able to put the letters in the mail before the mail delivery came. That's organized, and I believe myself to be unorganized, but maybe I am having a few thoughts that I am actually not so bad. I can be grateful for the little ways I make my life go smoothly.*

- *Today I decided not to sleep in. I got up and made my bed. When I came out of my bedroom with my bed all made like that, I felt accomplished and clean. I had the thought that I can do difficult things, that maybe things are getting a bit better. I felt a slight smile starting on my lips. My gratitude at getting up early warmed my chest.*

The more time you spend with these little victories, the more your brain will automatically focus on the good stuff when it happens.

Home Practice

Do your favorite mindfulness practice each day, whether it is Breathing Meditation, Standing Yoga, Body Scan, or Sitting Meditation. You can use your Mindfulness Playlist, or find something else that works for you. The more minutes you spend in mindfulness, the more easily your mind might focus on the present moment, even in informal mindfulness.

Near the end of each day, review Each Little Victory you can remember from your day. You can keep a list or just say them out loud to recognize your good work.

Writing Reflection

To stay focused on present goals and motivations, please review and rewrite your original intentions for TMS from Week Zero or write new ones if they have changed.

_____
_____
_____

Here are a couple of my Little Victories this week (things I am grateful for doing) because they are aligned with my values:

_____
_____
_____

Even if I don't like my present mood, I can still relate to it. I can be curious about what's showing up by:

_____
_____
_____

I can be grateful for myself by/because:

_____
_____
_____

Honoring the full range of my inner experiences means:

_____
_____
_____
_____

In my formal mindfulness practices recently, I have noticed:

_____
_____
_____
_____

This is different from how I used to relate to my inner experiences because:

_____
_____
_____

I can use this awareness to move in my chosen direction by:

_____
_____
_____
_____

Nature Connection

Gratitude For Each Little Thing

Immerse yourself in a natural setting and sit for a few minutes silently looking around you. Then start vocalizing your stream of consciousness about all the things around you that you are grateful for. They can be from so small you can't see them to large enough to encompass the earth. Please try your best to list at least 25. Then, when you have completed your spoken gratitude list, sit again, noticing what's happening inside of you.

Wise Words

"To educate yourself for the feeling of gratitude means to take nothing for granted, but to always seek out and value the kindness that will stand behind the action. Nothing that is done for you is a matter of course. Everything originates in a will for the good, which is directed at you. Train yourself never to put off the word or action for the expression of gratitude."

—Albert Schweitzer

"Stay . . . stay . . . just stay. Learning to stay with ourselves (in any mindful activity) is like training a dog. If we train a dog by beating it, we'll end up with an obedient but very inflexible and rather terrified dog. The dog may obey when we say "Stay!" "Come!" "Roll over!" and "Sit up!" but he will also be neurotic and confused. By contrast, training with kindness results in someone who is flexible and confident, who doesn't become upset when situations are unpredictable and insecure. So whenever we wander off, we gently encourage ourselves to "stay" and settle down. Are we experiencing restlessness? Stay! Discursive mind? Stay! Are fear and loathing out of control? Stay! Aching knees and throbbing back? Stay! What's for lunch? Stay! What am I doing here? Stay! I can't stand this another minute! Stay! That is how to cultivate steadfastness."

—Pema Chodron's Pith Instructions (permission from The Pema Chodron Foundation)

TMS Week Five

"Love creates a communion with life. Love expands us, connects us, sweetens us, ennobles us. Love springs up in tender concern, it blossoms into caring action. It makes beauty out of all we touch. In any moment we can step beyond our small self and embrace each other as beloved parts of a whole."

—JACK KORNFIELD

Being Whole and A Part of a System

You are well past halfway in your TMS treatment and six weeks into learning how to more mindfully consider your values and observe your own inner experiences, taking care to let go of judgment and practice being in the present moment. Wow. Your brain is changing and you are likely moving in the direction of a more meaningful life. Maybe you notice that you are more comfortable with TMS and your TMS team now. That comfort arises from showing up time and time again and being present. Maybe you are feeling better for the first time in a long while. Can you grow the good of that? What small measures of improvement or little victories can you notice: feeling lighter, more talkative, slightly more engaged in life? Maybe you are a bit more in touch with your own feelings and motivations? Maybe you notice your own responses are more in tune with those around you? Some participants experience small revelations about themselves or their lives during this week. Perhaps this comes from the magnetic stimulation and the way that the brain is being grown, or perhaps it comes from the many ways you are paying attention in the present moment. We know that with diligent practice, the brain is changing, and if you are getting results you intended, then keep doing what you have been doing. If you have not gotten much benefit, then talk about it with your team and pour on the mindfulness and self-support. The more steadily you practice, the more you are likely to change your brain.

By Week Five, TMS appointments are routine and you might notice that your brain automatically spends less energy anticipating, thinking about or remembering much about those TMS appointments. Week Five is a good time to check in with yourself or a support person or talk with your therapist about whether, now that the novelty of TMS treatment has worn off, you are still investing enough in your own effort to change your life. If you notice that your motivation to change has slipped a bit, perhaps you can intentionally bring an attitude of beginner's mind to some of what you are experiencing this week. There is still so much good for you to experience in the world!

If you have not had success eliminating depression, you may be having the thought that you want to give up, but please don't. What other thoughts could you invite in that might help you to feel more positive? What other aspects of your life could you call to mind that have improved even the slightest bit? It will be important to grow the good on whatever you see is changing in the direction of a more meaningful experience. And if your energy has slipped with your hopes, then how can you redouble your efforts to care for yourself by getting more active in the direction of your desired outcome? If you can find nothing that has changed, try employing an attitude of gratitude and beginner's mind to go through your behaviors with a fine-toothed comb to find some good. What did you use to do with the time you are now spending getting dressed, getting out of the house, interacting with your treatment team and spending constructive time supporting your treatment? That's a lot of self-care that you are doing now that you maybe didn't do before. No matter what depression is doing to you right now, you have the capacity to relate to it differently; indeed, you likely already are.

Some TMS participants who have more energy during Week Five notice feeling overwhelmed by all the things they are now thinking about wanting to change. Others find that this new energy from treatment has made them realize that a part or parts of their life (a relationship, job or lifestyle) no longer fit them as well. This insight can cause sadness and concern and can make a person feel pulled back toward depression as the person faces thoughts that "it might be too much work to change everything." And of course, some people are just able to enjoy their lives more by Week Five. No matter what is happening, it is always a great time to grow the good.

Understanding

Patient Acceptance and Action

During Week Five and beyond you can practice patient acceptance as you remind yourself that 1) you don't have to change everything in your life at once and 2) you might see tiny indications that you are (finally) moving in the direction you've wanted in your life. Isn't that why you committed so much toward TMS in the first place? You can always return to your values list to touch back in to your heartfelt motivation for living. Spend time tending to your body and listening to the experiences it is having as your body may be responding to changes in your inner environment. While paying mindful attention allows you to accept what is happening, acceptance does not mean you have to keep putting up with the discomfort. Acceptance might also mean that you can take action in a helpful way.

Here are some examples:

- *"I am having the thought that I can't stand my job and that's part of what depresses me . . . my value of working hard helps me remember that if I really need to change jobs eventually, I can do that, but right now, I want to keep feeling better . . . when I tune into my body, I can tend to the constriction I feel in my throat. When I take deep breaths and open my mouth to breathe, I feel better."*

- *"When I think about what's wrong at home, my heart starts racing and I feel difficulty catching my breath. This is depressing. . . . It's good for me to notice this pattern, and since my value of safety is not being met, I need to ask for some help to change that . . . When I tune into my body and notice the intense heartbeat, I can let my out-breath extend a bit to slow my pulse down. I can also get up and take a brisk walk to get the panicky feeling to subside a bit."*

- *"Now that I feel less numb, I have an overwhelming feeling of sadness. How am I supposed to be less depressed when I feel so sad? . . . my value of connection has been stymied by my mother's death last year, so I probably should look at that as part of the whole picture and at how our family system has been forced to change . . . I am going to work at letting myself cry when I feel like it, especially as I remember the last few times I spent with my mother."*

Love the Whole Body

As TMS treatment continues, regardless of what is happening inside right now, you can spend more time returning to your body as a refuge. Notice what's going on there and befriend *whatever* it is. From the body, you might notice that that brain of yours is running around, scanning the environment for the next big crisis. This is how our ancestors survived the many environmental and tribal challenges that came their way. Our brains haven't evolved fast enough to slow down in response to our much easier material lives. Now that you are paying attention, you can work with your whole body—including your brain—to experience the safety you *do* have and bring a bit of calm and ease into your present moment.

What would it be like to remind yourself of the safety, unconditional self-support and friendliness that we all have access to? There are so many ways to remind yourself, when appropriate:

- *"I am heading toward loving and accepting myself exactly as I am right now, and I am safe,"* or
- *"Whatever I am experiencing right now is already happening and I am OK,"* or
- *"I can lovingly be here now and watch what is happening as it happens. Nothing is threatening to me in this moment."*

Can you imagine yourself crouching down to a young child who is feeling scared or upset and softly reminding them that you see and care for them? Now, can you visualize crouching down to a young version of *yourself* who would benefit from the same reassurance? Before you move on to problem-solving, the soft touch of presence and loving-kindness is what grows feelings of safety and acceptance, a good start in solving any personal problem.

You Are Whole and Part of A System

As expressed above, you are *whole* and *safe* (unless, of course you are threatened and then it's important to work toward safety before anything else!) You can continue to remind yourself of this. It also sometimes becomes apparent that you are *also* part of a whole system that is bigger than you and that impacts you and influences what you do in the many realms of your life.

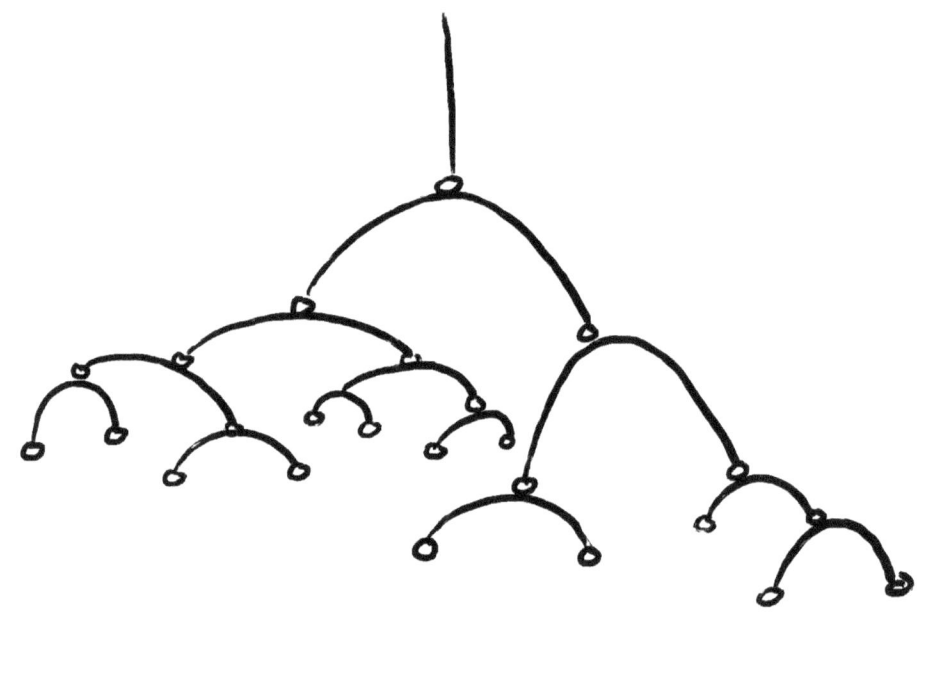

Think of a group you are part of—like your family, friends, or close work mates—as a mobile. Imagine that each person is a connected part and you all are both aligned in a variety of ways and also positioned in a fine balance. If you change an attribute of one of the parts, the whole mobile, by necessity, must shift. Depending on the integrity of the system, the whole thing might shift and still maintain a healthy balance. When the system is less functional in general, the integrity and balance of the whole mobile is disrupted and the mobile threatens to tip and tangle. (See Week Five Notes for more info on systems.)

If TMS and/or mindfulness changes how a person relates to their context—their mobile—then the other members of the system (family, friends, work mates) are connected such that it's reasonable to expect that some members will notice the impact of the change of balance. This change might cause personal experiences inside of them (thoughts, feelings, sensations, urges to action) in big or small ways that might cause further disruption to the hanging balance everyone was previously accustomed to. Sometimes the brains of the others in the system were so accustomed to the balance, they didn't even need to pay much attention to how the whole functioned; they could just maintain on autopilot.

For many people going through important transformation, like you might be with TMS treatment, it can be helpful to bring attention to the changes taking place, both internally and between members of the system. When you consider that you belong to several different mobiles or systems, you may find a lot to notice and navigate, but it's vital that you pay attention to all the systems to which you belong. How might you communicate to other members of your systems what your perceptions are? You have likely started to note those inner experiences for yourself, and perhaps now is a good time to learn to improve your communication with important others.

Take Your Time

This is all a lot of hard emotional work and can take time to shift. Remember that this learning belongs to a long process of change and does not need to be done immediately. This Mindfulness Sidekick is meant to accompany you well beyond your weeks in the TMS chair. If you are still at the stage of barely learning how to stay focused on your breath, then know that you have lots of time to share your innermost experiences and wants with beloved others. An attitude of patience, trust and generosity toward yourself will help you pace yourself through the information in this book.

You can start tuning in and paying attention at any point throughout your TMS journey, and change can happen anywhere along the way. To get maximum benefit out of TMS and this mindfulness business, you are hopefully talking with a mental health practitioner as you work on the the biggest factors that keep depression in place for you. Past experiences, family relationships, your role in other groups, or something else may keep you from moving along your path to a more meaningful life. Ideally, you are also sharing and comparing your experience with others, and practicing mindfulness activities as you go, to boost your capacity to navigate being part of a whole.

Skill to Try

Walking Meditation on your Mindfulness Sidekick Playlist

Walking Meditation is a practice that, like yoga, brings your body and breath into synchrony. You may find that you enjoy Walking Meditation because it allows you movement and space. It also represents symbolically the new path you are taking toward a more meaningful life. You will walk a small route for the duration of this recorded meditation, stopping and breathing deeply at the end of each stretch. Your anchor for awareness will be the bottom of each foot and your moving body.

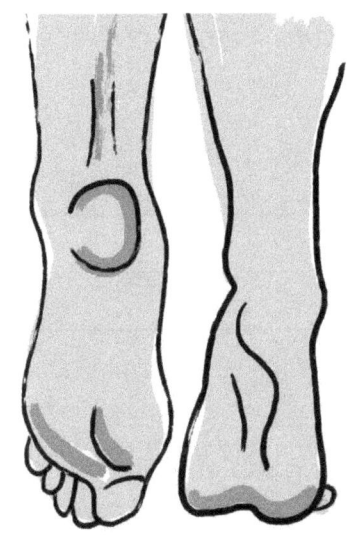

Writing Reflection

These are the values that inspired me to choose TMS treatment initially:
_____
_____
_____

I am part of the following groups:
_____
_____
_____
_____

These are the other people in my "mobile":
_____
_____
_____
_____

I am noticing that I am changing regarding:
_____
_____
_____
_____

I can notice a change in my relationship with_____.
I might be needing something different and the balance of our relationship is different because:

_____
_____
_____
_____

In order not to take on too much, this is what I can observe and this is what I can commit to:

_____
_____
_____
_____
_____

During the walking meditation, I noticed:

_____
_____
_____
_____
_____

This is not my usual walking! Walking meditation allowed me to:

_____
_____
_____

I am starting to really notice the patterns of my mind. Here's what I observe about my thoughts, sensations and feelings regarding something powerful or important in my life:

_____
_____
_____
_____

Knowing how my mind works might help me to take care of myself by:

_____
_____
_____
_____

When I stay in my body, I can:

_____
_____
_____
_____

Nature Connection

Walk among the trees or bushes near where you spend time. As you walk, notice not only the steps you are making, but also the plants alongside of you. Let your hands hang down and touch the plants as you pass. Every so often, pause, look up at the sky above you or in the distance and take a deep breath in, just noticing. Feel the connection between you and the green living beings around you. Notice and imagine the ways these living beings depend upon and live in community with one another. Sense into the idea that you are whole and good and that you are also a part of this living community.

Wise Words

"As a single footstep will not make a path on the earth, so a single thought will not make a pathway in the mind. To make a deep physical path, we walk again and again. To make a deep mental path, we must think over and over the kind of thoughts we wish to dominate our lives."

—Henry David Thoreau

TMS Week Six

"What I want in my life is compassion, a flow between myself and others based on a mutual giving from the heart."

—MARSHALL B. ROSENBERG

Acting Discerningly, Communicating Compassionately

At the beginning of this week, you will have attended 25 TMS treatment sessions, and will have spent at least 500 minutes with the magnet stimulating growth in your limbic system, connecting your emotional center with your rational thinking centers and being pulled by that magnet into a different life for your brain. Add to that number the minutes you have spent in transit to your appointments as you anticipated change and grew the good of your treatments afterward, thanking yourself for your present service to your future self. Anyone can see that you are dedicated to getting well. Congratulations on having already taken so many steps forward on your path toward emotional well-being and a life that you want! Have you ever really showed up for yourself like you are during this treatment? Arriving at Week Six—in and of itself—is a victory. It signifies that you are capable of changing your routine, withstanding discomfort in various forms, and taking action to solve a problem. Your actions testify to your faith in a better life.

You might be getting tired of this book cheering you on, talking about what an accomplishment each week is, but shouldn't you be given accolades? Anecdotal evidence might show you that experiencing gratitude and growing the good helps you to feel a bit better, and you deserve it.

You can try now by taking another deep breath and bringing to mind something good and important you recognize you have done since Week Zero. Watch as thoughts come in. Are they enhancing positivity or stealing it? Do the thoughts coming in bring pride or shame? Your capacity for mindfulness allows you just to observe what's taking place in that mind of yours, to learn the pattern of your own thoughts and to bring friendliness, or self-compassion. This might feel different; these thoughts that you are observing are real but they are not The Truth; they are just pictures or combinations of words that have slid through your mind often enough so there's a nice neural pathway for a thought to slide easily through again, like a sled slips down a snow-covered hill, making a track for the next time it slides down. Can you perceive these thoughts as just passing stimuli? Can watching the thoughts slip by now allow you to stay here with ease, to create the awareness that arises when you are not regretting the past, judging the present, or planning for the future? And with your next breath, can you invite a thought, again, of something you have done these last weeks and bring friendliness with it? Try thanking your past self for what you've done for your future self.

Because these brains of ours are designed to search for the next potential problem, we can easily lose that friendliness with ourselves. As we pay attention to the ways we are taking good care so that problems are less likely to happen, we can observe the passing stimuli of warnings and deal with what is happening in this moment. So, as you check in with how you are feeling in the start of Week Six and realize you are feeling well, but having the thought that "this feeling won't last" or that "some dreadful surprise is around the corner," you can thank your brain for that thought and return your focus back to the actions you are taking now, to be well.

Around this week, you might notice feelings of anxiousness or fear. You might perceive sensations of a racing heart, tightness in your jaw or a heavy brow. These stimuli are important to pay attention to, not because they are problems that need to be fixed, but because then you know you are awake and aware, in awareness. With extended mindfulness practice, the amygdala (alarm center for fear in the limbic system) shrinks, the prefrontal cortex (aware, executive functioning part of the brain) grows, and the functional connections between the amygdala and the prefrontal cortex are strengthened. This leads to less reactivity, and attention and concentration improve. The uncomfortable feelings you've tried to get rid of might be diminishing as a byproduct of mindful attention—hooray!

Understanding

Letting Go

The mindful attitude of letting go here means letting your heart race *and* keeping attention on the minute details—letting yourself get forensically curious—staying, paying attention, observing what is happening in this very second... and this second... and this second, and not taking action to fix the problem of what you are sensing. You are not letting go of the sensation per se, rather *letting go of trying to fix the sensation*.

By Week Six, if you've been cultivating your own formal mindfulness practice, you may also be "having the thought that," yes, you are having thoughts and watching them slip by and that this experience feels different than being bombarded with thoughts and needing to change them. You may also be spontaneously developing more feelings of acceptance and self-compassion or loving-kindness from so much friendly watching and non-striving and so little fixing. Perhaps that self-acceptance is even leading you to sensations of openness and warmth that feel more comfortable than before. This change is always possible.

But Don't Let Your Self Go

With all this encouragement to observe, you might have the thought that you are not supposed to DO anything, ever. Of course, this is not advised if you want to move along the path to your most meaningful life. Your mindfulness practice is helping you to discern when to act and how to act to bring benefit to yourself, others, and the world. Here are some examples of such discernment:

- *You notice feelings of anger at someone you know well. Your mindfulness training helps you to watch the feelings build up inside you, heat up your face, clench your hands and host dozens of sleds down your snow-covered mind hill ("He doesn't care about me." "I am getting out of here now." "I'd like to make him cry." "He doesn't deserve to be here." "Why have I done this to myself?") You do not act out of anger. You do something that allows you to stay with your attention on what's in front of you—like breathing deeply or telling yourself that you are safe or feeling your feet rooted into the floor—and you don't act. You let time pass until your nervous system has calmed and you are again thinking clearly enough to communicate compassionately, to work toward being understood and solving the cause of your anger.*

- *You feel embarrassed because you failed to do an important task in your work. Instead of making up an excuse to feel relief, you pause to let the ears-on-fire and heart-sinking sensations build in intensity, (ooh, this feels awful!) They eventually (after too, too long!) subside, as you watch—but not subscribe to—your thoughts ("I am so stupid." "They are going to be so mad." "I hate this darn job anyway." "I am going to get fired.") Once you are less physically impacted by this embarrassment, you speak with your supervisor to admit your mistake and apologize, taking deep breaths and reminding yourself that what you did was human, and not so bad.*

- *You worry that you won't be able to show up to the family holiday because you have been feeling so low. You hear yourself hurling unkind words at yourself, berating yourself for your mood and your lack of holiday cheer. You notice the thoughts ("You are a loser, you can't hack being with family." "People are going to be mad at you for not showing up and they'll talk badly about you." "You will never be able to visit family like a normal person.") You take slow, deep breaths as you try to focus on your body breathing. You wait until the strongest storm of negative thoughts is over and then you act in self-support, telling yourself empathic statements and wrapping your arms around yourself in a gesture of comfort and protection. Then you call your sister, who is hosting, to explain that you are not feeling up to joining the family this time and you spend your time resting and repeating the breathing and self-talk that helps a bit.*

Discerning Action

Living with symptoms of depression is already difficult enough. Wouldn't it be easier to bring curiosity, relaxation and acceptance to what you are experiencing rather than to insult yourself or react in other unhelpful ways? Ideally, TMS has decreased your symptoms of depression. (You can look back at the symptom cloud in the Introduction chapter to see what's changed.) Your regular mindfulness practice will open you to noticing what is and discerning what helps, so that you can choose your focus and take committed action to move you forward on the path toward your more meaningful life.

It's also possible that the same severity of depression symptoms still plagues you. Though this is not the outcome you want (and please don't give up hope, there still plenty of time for your brain to respond to TMS), your mindful attention can change how you are relating to these pesky symptoms and will help you take committed action anyway:

- *Alicia finds that though she is tired, instead of taking that as a "stop sign," she does all her laundry anyway because she will feel better having done the laundry than having the thought over and over again "I still have to do my laundry, darn it." And she can then enjoy her fresh, clean clothes.*
- *When Alex gets agitated, instead of beating himself up for not being more patient, he might acknowledge impatience and then act as if he is patient, exploring what that feels like on the inside. Eventually, what he is wanting to be over will be.*
- *If Linda is having difficulty remembering things, instead of getting upset and declaring this the beginning of a bigger problem, she notes the problem happening and asks for help from her partner to remember the important things. With loving-kindness and better reminder techniques, she'll get to focus on recovering from depression so that her memory itself improves, and if it doesn't, she will use more advanced strategies in the future.*

Discerning Action with Thoughts

How can you tell whether a thought is workable on this journey to your best life? If you're not sure, you can ask yourself:

- Does it help me to be the person I want to be?
- Does it help me to build the sort of relationships I'd like?
- Does it help me to connect with what I truly value?
- Does it help me to make the most of my life as it is in this moment?
- Does it help me to take effective action to change my life for the better?
- Does it help me, in the long term, to create a rich, full and meaningful life?

If the answer to any of these questions is yes, then you might make friends with this thought and invite it back. If the answer to all of them is no, then the thought is not workable. This is the time to change your focus to a more workable thought or action so that you can grow your mind out of that unworkable thought as best you can. What you know will grow, so think about how your are tending your garden of the mind!

When you get more curious and bring nonjudment and are able to just observe and take discerning action, what do you notice happening? How is this in accordance with your values and the life you are wanting to lead? How do you imagine you, specifically, might be impacted by less self-judgment and more self-compassion, generosity and gratitude? You might want to take a minute here and visualize or sense into what it might be like to embody more of those warm qualities.

Sometimes Treatment Changes Our Perspective

Because we are such social beings, we often have multiple relationships, and eventually something arises that causes us to have something important about us to communicate with another person in our lives. During TMS treatment, you might recognize that you are changing in ways you had hoped, and you want to affirm that change and keep up momentum in that desired direction. In Week Five, you learned about how the balance in any group of people in your life (family members, work mates, friends, etc.), no matter how small, might shift as you change. In order to reestablish balance, you have two choices: you could stop changing and stay the same or you could change. If you decide that you don't want to stay the same and you want to change, it might become vital to communicate information to another person so that they understand what is going on and how they might take a role in supporting you. While most people will welcome your transformation away from depression symptoms, important others can sometimes feel threatened by the change they see. Speaking with clarity and compassion might create greater harmony. Compassionate Communication, an approach to non-violent communication (created by Marshall Rosenberg and originally called Nonviolent Communication),[1] shines important light on the idea that most human behavior is an attempt to meet our universal human needs and that we get out of balance when our attempts to get our needs met clashes with another's attempts at the same. Compassionate Communication helps us to (mindfully) identify our needs, and in communicating them to another we are acknowledging the needs and affirming our ability to take some small action. Ideally the other person communicates in this way as well and the two can recognize their commonality and move to collaborate, so that the needs of both people can move toward being met. If this can happen, then a value toward interpersonal harmony might not be far off, and both people will have learned more about the other and themselves.

Compassionate Communication is a mindfulness practice in that a practitioner perceives what is observable and shares that without doing more, and the approach thrives with many of the same attitudes that support mindfulness.

No matter how many times you've suffered with an interpersonal conflict, bringing an attitude of **beginner's mind** *can help you observe anew and get you out of the reactive pattern of your past with this person.*

No one likes to feel criticized, so **nonjudging** *greases the wheels for you to roll toward the solution of peaceful collaboration. The listener will be less likely to feel defensive, more likely to lower their shoulders and open their ears, showing willingness to learn from what you have observed.*

While **trust** *might be one of the most difficult attitudes to foster, perhaps you can breathe more deeply knowing that you are the best witness to your own experience. Believing in yourself as you communicate can help your listener trust you. While you may have the thought that you* should *be thinking, feeling, sensing, or doing, letting go allows you to be exactly as you are and to communicate exactly what you know, without being hamstrung by the expectations of both yourself and another.*

Speaking your **gratitude** *for the listener might open the hearts of both people for more receptivity and better listening.*

It might be a lot to expect that people in your life are ready for collaborating by using Compassionate Communication, so you can start with your own education and communications to others without expecting to be met with the same. Often during TMS treatment, participants realize that people in their lives are curious about how they are doing with TMS and whether it's helping alleviate depression. This is a good chance to practice communicating simple observation, to share with others what's happening as a result of this constellation of treatment and practice. For example:

- *"I am noticing that I have more energy to ask for more of your attention."*
- *"Wow. This treatment process is feeling intense for me. I am mostly concerned for my well-being right now."*
- *"I have a little bit of hope now that I didn't have before. I feel closer to you now that I am not worrying about myself quite as much."*
- *"Now that I am feeling a bit better, I am getting more angry at people, and I want to try to make sense of that anger so that I can express it in a way that will be respectful to you."*
- *"I feel grateful that I have some more positive thoughts than I used to."*
- *"I have the urge to pull myself into a cocoon lately; I want to conserve my energy."*
- *"I am happy that I notice having enough energy to stay up with you because it's meaningful time for me."*

These single statements can express details to help connect you with another. In addition to encouraging self-observation, Compassionate Communication provides a helpful framework to expand direct and friendly communication to situations where you'd like someone to understand you better, and even do something different to help you meet a universal need. Here are the four aspects we can share when we use Compassionate Communication:

1. **What we are observing.** Observations are made from a place of non-judgment, nonevaluation and noninterpretation. They are value-neutral statements based on our hearing or seeing, or on inarguable, non-subjective facts.

Example:

> Judgment: "You're cruel!" Observation: "When you said I look like crap..."
>
> Judgment: "I hate men!" Observation: "When you yelled, 'Oooo, Hot Mama' at that woman..."

2. **The sensations we are experiencing** in our bodies and the **feelings** we understand ourselves to be having as a result of what we are observing. Feelings are not perceptions but rather attempts to describe how the current thought or situation is affecting me physically. They are represented by feeling words only (sad, unsure, excited, surprised, etc.) and not an expression of "I feel like..." because that is a thought rather than a feeling. Sensations link us to our bodies, which are receptors of present moment experience. (See page 47 for a sensations list). Sensations in our bodies help us to make sense of our present situation.

3. **What we are wanting or needing** (similar to what we value). Needs/values motivate and sustain us rather than what we think we "should" be doing. (See page 27 for a values list.)

Example:

> Judgment: "I don't know why I put up with you, anyway!" Need: "I really want more respect, but I also want to know why you said that."
>
> Judgment: "Our lives would be so much better without them." Need: "My need for unity and peace is not getting met right now."

4. **What we hope for from the listener.** It's not always necessary to communicate #4, but it is vital if you want the listener to do something different, and they don't happen to read minds! These requests invite your listener, and are doable, specific actions, rather than a request to refrain from doing something. Holding the request lightly protects you from experiencing disconnection if the listener declines. Your self-knowledge

about your own best care does not depend on the listener saying yes to your request. And knowing ourselves well allows us to find alternate ways to meet those needs.[2]

Here are five different Compassionate Communication statements in the context of family, with statements 1-4 in different orders for workability.

#1

Observation:	"I hear you say you won't come home tonight until you have finished all that you have to do at work . . .
Feeling:	. . . and I'm feeling some frustration and disappointment.
Needs/values:	It's important to me that our family has some time at home together because I am feeling more energetic from treatment and want to make up for a bit of lost time.
Request:	Would you tell me what's preventing you from coming home earlier so that we could have an easy relaxing evening and play a game with the kids? Thank you."

#2

Feeling:	"I feel irritated . . .
Observation:	. . . when I see you've left dishes all over the counter and remember that we had an agreement to take turns cleaning up.
Request:	Would you clean it up before we go to bed?

Needs/values:	I want to trust that I can enjoy waking up in the morning and coming out to the kitchen, seeing it's clean and being able to relax. Thanks."

#3

Needs/values:	"Because sharing responsibility is important to me as a parent and I've learned I can't do it all by myself . . .
Request:	. . . would you finish your chores while I set the table?
Feeling:	I'm grateful . . .
Observation:	. . . seeing what you've already done today to help me here at home. You walked the dogs and did your laundry and your room is decently clean—thank you!"

#4

Observation:	"I'm hearing your invitation to go to a movie after dinner tonight . . .
Feeling:	. . . and I'm feeling so exhausted and a bit sad, so . . .
Needs/values:	. . . I'd rather rest and take a bubble bath.
Request:	Could we have a rain check? Thanks for understanding."

#5

Request:	"Would you be willing to take me to the airport this afternoon?

Feeling: I'm feeling somewhat anxious . . .

Needs/values: . . . and I could use some support and help.

Observation: My car hasn't been running well this week and I don't think I can do everything I've put on my plate right now. I'd feel grateful."

Compassionate Communication is a kind of mindfulness practice because when a person communicates in this way, they can focus less on judging and more on clarifying what is being observed, experienced, and valued. Rosenberg states, "We are dangerous when we are not conscious of our responsibility for how we behave, think, and feel," and so Compassionate Communication allows us to "shine the light of consciousness on places where we can hope to find what we are seeking."[2] As with mindfulness, Compassionate Communication skills are different enough from what you've likely grown up with that it takes lots of practice reps for the brain to use the techniques smoothly. (For more information, please visit www.nonviolentcommunication.com and see Week Six, #3,4.)

Skill to Try

Listening Meditation on your Mindfulness Sidekick Playlist

Follow Rumi's observation that "The quieter you become the more you are able to hear." Get as quiet as you can and listen to the sounds around you. Eventually you can stop using the guided meditation and just listen mindfully wherever and whenever.

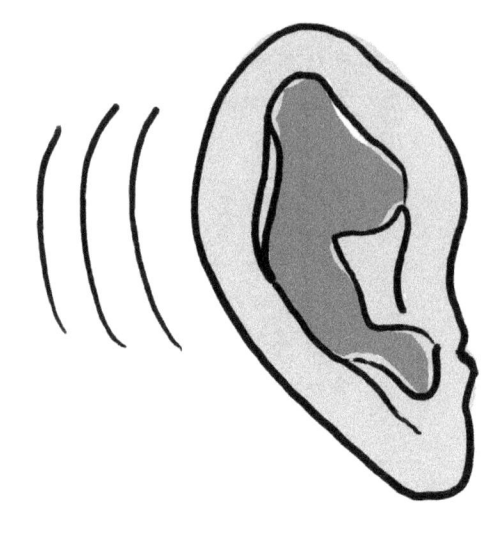

Home Practice

Practice the Listening Meditation each day, notice specifically when and how you can manage to listen so deeply when another is talking.

Share at least one Compassionate Communication statement per day with someone who will honor you by listening as Rumi would have them do. Use statements #1-4 above to help guide you. Even if you are clumsy, paper in hand, stumbling on the words, feeling robotic and self-conscious, doing it anyway will help you learn. You'll get smoother with practice, and the pattern of communication will start to make sense as it moves you further on your path to your more meaningful life.

Participate once a day in whatever other mindfulness practice (Yoga, Body Scan, Sitting Meditation, Walking Meditation) propels you along that same desired path.

Writing Reflection

I might try out this Compassionate Communication with _____ because:

_____

_____

_____

Here's how it might sound:

Observation: ("When I see/hear/experience . . .")

_____

_____

_____

Feeling: ("I feel . . ." *insert feeling word here, <u>not</u> thought, often expressed with 'I feel like . . .'*)

_____

_____

_____

Values/Needs: ("Because I value/need. . .")

_____

_____

_____

Request: ("Would you be willing to . . .")

_____
_____
_____

You can also have a conversation with yourself that moves you to act in a way that supports your own well-being. Check in about how you experience this when you have finished the below exercise.

Observation: ("When I see/hear/experience . . .")

_____
_____
_____

Feeling: ("I feel. . ." *insert feeling words here, not thoughts*)

_____
_____
_____

Values/Needs: ("Because I value/need . . .")

_____
_____
_____

Request: ("I'd like to . . .")

_____
_____
_____

Your mindfulness practice is only in its infancy and the more you keep attending to the emotions, thoughts and sensations that you now are having, the stronger the practice grows. You are not training to change those inner experiences, rather you are training to change your relationship with them. If your inner experience of depression has not diminished, then how has your relationship with those inner experiences changed, if at all? Whether TMS has lessened depression yet or not, the control you have is over how you relate to your inner experiences and how often you practice mindfulness. What are your observations about relating to any mood state lately?

You can communicate with that mood state or with depression in general using Compassionate Communication. Tell it what you'd like it to know and ask for what you need from it.

Observation: ("Hey, Depression, when I see/hear/experience . . .")

_____
_____
_____

Feeling: ("I feel . . ." *remember—a feeling word, not "I feel like . . ."*)

_____
_____
_____

Values/Needs: ("Because I value/need . . .")

_____

_____

_____

Request: ("Depression, would you be willing to . . .")

_____

_____

_____

The more you practice Compassionate Communication, the more you might see your own self more clearly (and forgive yourself for just being human!) and the more clarity you may have to collaborate with others, to feel close and to regain balance in your relationships.

Nature Connection

Find a favorite natural living thing growing near you. Go there every day for a week or so and do something to tend to it, (weeding around it, watering it, placing it out of harms' way, breathing on it, talking to it, etc.). Each day, share at least one Compassionate Communication thought with this living being, the object of your attention. Do this each day, paying attention to what happens inside you over the following days.

Wise Words

"My theory is that we get depressed because we're not getting what we want, and we're not getting what we want because we have never been taught to get what we want. Instead, we've been taught to be good little boys and girls and good mothers and fathers. If we're going to be one of those good things, better get used to being depressed. Depression is the reward we get for being "good." But, if you want to feel better, I'd like you to clarify what you would like people to do to make life more wonderful for you."

—Marshall Rosenberg, *Nonviolent Communication: A Language of Life*

TMS Week Seven

"By giving ourselves unconditional kindness and comfort while embracing the human experience, difficult as it is, we avoid destructive patterns of fear, negativity, and isolation."

—KRISTIN NEFF

Cultivating Loving-Kindness

You are like a marathon runner who persists in moving ahead on this road, knowing that the finish line is near and perhaps sensing the fortitude you've tapped into to keep going. You have finished the main course of TMS and now you're likely receiving just a few taper sessions this week. Maybe you are noticing feelings of independence as you have thoughts about how soon treatment will end. And . . . you might be noticing emotions and thoughts that you did not expect to have at this point in treatment. Some who are experiencing the desired results—fewer and less severely depressed mood states—from TMS might notice feelings of excitement and hope mixed with fear or worry and the thought that "Good stuff never lasts for me." Some who are not yet feeling great might notice emotions of disappointment, hopelessness, even regret, and the thought that TMS is disappointing or that they themselves are "unfixable." If you are having negative and difficult thoughts about yourself, Week Seven is an important chance to practice self-compassion, or loving-kindness, and to see what happens inside of you.

Perhaps no matter what is taking place in there, you are noticing your mind wandering off when you intend to pay attention; this happens naturally for people already, and especially when those people find themselves in a transition. The brain turns attention towards novelty, making it difficult to sustain focus on any one thing for too long. You may feel bored with or tired of working so laboriously to improve your mood. Or . . . if you feel good, you may have (wishful) thoughts that your mental health had improved so much that you no longer need to work so diligently to feel well. These thoughts signal an opening to redouble your efforts to keep going on your desired path, working with mindfulness and acting according to your values all the more.

Real change can happen; regardless of what thoughts are arising, it matters what you DO. Your brain grows what it knows, so if you want to grow joy, practice joy by doing things you love. If you want to grow calm, put yourself in situations where you feel peaceful and grow the good. If you want to minimize loneliness, do activities to connect with others in meaningful ways. If you want to feel loving-kindness for yourself, practice loving-kindness. As all gardeners know, you harvest that which you plant and tend.

By now, you are probably aware of how easily critical thoughts about yourself or others show up, even when things are going decently, but especially when success is nowhere to be found. The question to ask yourself is: is such disapproval workable? In other words, does denunciation help you move forward on your path to a chosen, more meaningful life, or does it weigh you down and slow your progress? What has criticizing yourself or others ever given you? Does it enhance your sense that you are good and whole? If your answers reveal that criticism does nothing for you, then the practice of loving-kindness—friendliness, goodwill or mercy that arises from love—might change the climate of your inner experiences enough for something new to grow. A more gentle and loving inner environment might prepare you well for the post-TMS phase of your journey, but you must be the one to judge that!

Understanding

Loving-kindness meditation, as an aspect of mindfulness practice, has been shown to increase positive emotions, decrease negative emotions and strengthen a sense of purpose in life.[1] Loving-kindness meditation has also been shown to reduce depression and PTSD symptoms,[2] increase peoples' sense of well-being and compassion toward themselves,[3] strengthen compassion toward others[4] and reduce self-criticism.[5]

What would those changes be like for you? Refreshing? Freeing? Motivating? With this potential help from loving-kindness, let's get on to the simple practice below.

Skills to Try

Skill One: Loving-Kindness Meditation on your Mindfulness Sidekick Playlist

Loving-Kindness Meditation is a specific type of mindfulness meditation that focuses on cultivating compassion. It involves evoking a series of positive well-wishes for the well-being of oneself and others. It is also referred to as the Loving-Kindness Prayer because its structure is like an intercessory prayer. This mindfulness practice provides a way of moving toward warmth, compassion and caring for oneself and others and away from negativity and criticism.

The practice can begin with focusing positive well-wishes toward yourself, then someone who has been kind or helpful to you, then someone about whom you've felt neutral, then someone whom you love, then someone with whom you may have difficulty and then with all beings. Though this is the way this Mindfulness Sidekick Playlist's meditation progresses, you can send this friendly compassion to anyone or any group of people you choose as you progress to doing this on your own. This form of loving-kindness meditation, in particular, is based on the Tibetan Buddhist prayer for compassion and is close to one written by Jack Kornfield.[6]

> May I be filled with loving-kindness.
> May I be well in body and mind.
> May I be safe from every danger.
> May I be at ease and happy.

Skill Two: Lying Down Yoga on your Mindfulness Sidekick Playlist

During this Yoga session, you might experiment with applying loving-kindness and gratitude toward your body. Gently note the objections your mind may make and focus on bringing the attitudes of love and kindness to your yoga movements and your breath. If "love" and "kindness" are too big, how about "friendliness?"

Home Practice

Write the four lines of the Loving-Kindness Meditation seen above—or some version of your choosing—on a card to carry with you so that you can pull it out when you need it. You could also make a second copy to post at home, at work or in your car.

Practice this meditation for self-compassion daily. Even if it feels strange, keep working with it for as many stanzas as you can (i.e. with loved ones, strangers, even "enemies.")

Choose one activity daily among all your options: Standing Yoga, Lying Down Yoga, Walking Meditation, Body Scan, Sitting Meditation. Acknowledge moments you are able to sustain the effort at this activity and let go of moments you space out, give up or criticize yourself. This learning is a process, and if you can keep trying to bring loving-kindness to those moments of disappointment, you are already doing the behavior of building compassion!

Writing Reflection

When I recite my loving-kindness well-wishes, I notice in my body that:
_____
_____
_____

When I practice those friendly well-wishes, I notice I have the thought that:
_____
_____
_____

When I say those warm well-wishes, I notice I have feelings such as:
_____
_____
_____

The lesson I want to take from this practice of loving-kindness is:
_____
_____
_____

This practice of compassion might improve my mental wellness because:

_____
_____
_____

Generally these days, I am noticing:

_____
_____
_____

What I am noticing is different than it used to be because:

_____
_____
_____

Focused attention trained on what is happening changes my relationship with what is happening because:

_____
_____
_____

Nature Connection

Bring friendly loving-kindness to a living being in nature that you can spend time with. For example, if a mountain you can see in the distance is the object of your attention, then start with some phrases of loving-kindness toward the mountain. You can make them up as you go: "May you sit still and tall as the sun rises and sets./May you be covered with animals who live on you./May you never have drilling or blasting in you." Let your heart lead your words and follow your heart as it opens and connects with the natural object of your attention, however big or small.

Wise Words

Christian Loving-Kindness Prayer

> May I experience God's mercy
> May I experience God's peace
> May I experience God's love

(this can be said for others by inserting the appropriate subject pronoun)

"Using the body as a whole as the object of your attention in lying-down meditation is a blessing. You can feel the body from head to toe, breathing and radiating warmth over the entire envelope of your skin. It's the whole body that breathes, the whole body that is alive. In bringing mindfulness to the body as a whole, you can reclaim your entire body as the locus of your being and your vitality, reminding yourself that "you," whoever you are, are not just a resident of your head."

—Jon Kabat-Zinn, *Wherever You Go There You Are*

TMS Week Eight

"Too much of one thing can end up creating stress; this is something that no one needs in their life. But living a life in balance can provide harmony and peace."

—CATHERINE PULSIFER

"The key is not to prioritize what's on your schedule, but to schedule your priorities."

—STEPHEN COVEY

Scheduling Your Time

Welcome to Week Eight! About two months have passed since you likely first opened The Mindfulness Sidekick. Do you remember what you first experienced as you began these pages—what thoughts, feelings and sensations arose back then? The end of this week marks two months since the first time you sat in the TMS chair. Can you recall the feelings you had as you started treatment? As you reach back into what was then unknown about the short-term future that has by now revealed itself, what do you find surprising? What are you proud of that you started doing two months ago as you set out on this journey to improve your mental health? What actions have increased your degree of wellness? What behavior do you wish you had started doing two months ago so that today it might be a habit? With so many questions to be pondered, perhaps you are feeling energetic enough to delve into them. If you are not feeling lively in this way, please bring loving-kindness to that part of yourself that is keeping you from doing so. Can you pay attention to what that part might be saying with its resistance? Remember that you can always return to examine these questions later, when you choose to.

With likely only a couple of taper sessions a week now, TMS is not filling your calendar as it was. You might notice that you are making time for new behaviors that help support changes for the better—good work! You might also notice, maybe with disappointment, that these new windows of time are spent doing things you don't value, such as worrying, procrastinating tasks, drinking, smoking marijuana, or scrolling social media. What does nonjudgmental noticing look like, while still bringing your attention to how the actions you are noticing might not be behaviors that lead you on your path to your most meaningful life?

Week Eight is a good time to turn your focus to a short-term schedule to support long-term recovery from depression. If you don't yet have a clear design for sustained brain and life change, this week is a good time to create a preliminary one. If you do have a longer term plan, Week Eight is ideal for reviewing the plan and sharing it with a trusted support person beyond your TMS treatment team. Friends will see your grit when you show them what you plan to do and will also likely be relieved to know how they might specifically be helpful. Mental health *practitioners usually love it when a client arrives at their session with a plan of action, and they will likely be ready to collaborate with you to make those intentions a reality.*

Regardless of how you are feeling this week, you may notice thoughts of self-judgment arising. What can you do with these beyond noticing them? With diligent loving-kindness as you practiced in Week Seven, perhaps you can move ahead with your planning even though you don't feel exactly as you'd like to feel . . . yet. When you bring warm friendliness to whatever critical or downer voice is talking inside of you, do you notice any tiny thing happening for the better?

As with every other brain training technique, well-constructed neuropathways are not built in a day, especially when you have to dismantle a self-critical mental highway system! Just . . . keep . . . practicing. You may also notice emotions resulting from either met or unmet needs, as you learned through Compassionate Communication in TMS Week Six. Regardless of what you are or aren't doing, self-compassion is key to sustained motivation. You will *make mistakes and you* can *pick yourself back up and try again.*

Going back to the simple mindfulness basics can be helpful. Remember that mindfulness is the awareness that arises when we pay attention on purpose, nonjudgmentally. What can you notice—thoughts, feelings, sensations—and how can you cultivate friendly, nonjudgmental presence this week? As time goes by, you might be moving more fully into your most meaningful life, making choices based on what you know works best for you. What small steps do you want to take in these last two weeks before you complete TMS treatment and continue moving on your path into the future?

Writing down your thoughts will likely be helpful (below). Taking one minute, one hour, one day at a time aids in establishing the habits and attitudes of this post-TMS life. If you have been working through The Mindfulness Sidekick *consistently, you have spent enough time with mindfulness to know what works well for your own mental health. Practice what you already know to be workable and healthy for you; if it's good, do more of it, more often and more regularly!*

Please continue to build your support network; your TMS treatment team will be available for a few more sessions and then your practitioner might be accessible when you make appointments after treatment, but everyone needs at least a couple true supporters to help keep positive change going. We are inherently social creatures, and our minds thrive when championed by other empathic minds.

Understanding

The Healthy Mind Platter[1]

The Healthy Mind Platter is a concept for healthy living introduced by interpersonal neurobiologist Dr. Dan Siegel and neuroleadership expert Dr. David Rock that was modeled after the healthy eating plate unveiled by the US government in 2011 to encourage a balanced intake of foods. Drs. Siegel and Rock's graphic depicts seven neurocognitive activities that nurture the mind and can be partaken every day. When a person determines (by unscientific trial and error, mostly) how much of each "ingredient" they require to cultivate and maintain their optimal mental health, then they have an easier time knowing what proportions to "serve themselves" on any given day or week, using variety and complementarity (i.e. not only sleep and focused work, for example) to find healthy balance.

The Healthy Mind Platter

The Healthy Mind Platter for Optimal Brain Matter. Copyright © 2011 David Rock and Daniel J. Siegel, M.D. All rights reserved. Used with permission.

Please look at the Healthy Mind Platter and consider your own daily and weekly routine. What ingredients do you have plenty of? What elements are missing? You do not have to spend equal amounts of time at each activity, but you might want to add in the aspects that are lacking and boost ingredients that bring you the most robust sense of well-being. Your specific schedule will look different from others around you, depending on what your needs are.

For example:

> Emily likes to be very active (physical time), even in the rainy winter in Oregon. Jose prefers to do a minimum of exercise but feels most alive when working on the computer he is building (focus time). Emily and Jose would require different amounts of movement time and focused time in their lives to achieve optimal mental health. But if Jose never exercised (physical time), he would be missing his best mix of activity

for his own mental wellness. Jose could schedule times in his week when he can get up and move his body to improve his physical health and stimulate the release of feel-good brain chemicals. Since Emily works for UPS and is walking, lifting and climbing constantly for her work, she might benefit from making time to slow down and tune into what's happening inside herself (time in).

Of course, most people already spend some necessary hours focusing for work or caring for family and hours sleeping; which of the "times" might you add into your schedule to improve balance in your own life? There are many questions that can guide your planning, including:

- *Does it help to spend this time earlier or later in the day?*
- *Could you spend this time with or near others who will make it more palatable?*
- *Of the ingredients you seem to be missing or low on, is there some location that would help you do any of the activities?*
- *Are there any materials or equipment you could acquire that would encourage you to spend time cultivating this necessary ingredient?*

There are many scheduling apps for your phone that might help you organize your time, and a paper plan awaits you as an example that you might fill out to get started on making sure that all your healthy mind ingredients can be a part of your regular weekly activities.[2] You don't have to accomplish time in each category each day, but making time for each category within the week might contribute to your sense of balance and well-being.

You might also consider sharing your thoughts and intentions with your therapist or with one of your support people. You might know someone who is accustomed to keeping their time organized through scheduling and they might have ideas for you, including ways to avoid normal pitfalls and obstacles to staying planful. Whether your mind needs time focusing, playing, connecting, moving, being mellow, introspecting or sleeping, with some creative time engineering, you can move toward fitting it all into a better life balance!

Home Practice

Choose one mindfulness activity each day. (You can count that for *time in*!) After you practice, spend some time writing (focus time!) about whatever you are noticing. When you read what you've written, please give yourself time to reread and compassionately affirm what you are experiencing by using words like "I can accept this" and "Just thoughts, coming and going" and "Good job listening to your body!" Notice, especially, when you can affirm that you are noticing uncomfortable or unwanted experiences.

Bring attention to your breath in your everyday activities as often as you remember. Practice pausing, or slowing your body down and breathing in and out deeply, unhurriedly. Then just pick up where you left off in your activity, paying renewed attention to what you are doing.

Repeat self-compassionate statements when you need them. You can either make up what seems appropriate in the moment, or repeat the wishes you read and practiced during Week Seven.

> May I be filled with loving-kindness.
> May I be safe from inner and outer dangers.
> May I be well in body and mind.
> May I be at ease and happy.

Writing Reflection

Among focus time, play time, connecting time, physical time, down time, time in, or sleep time, I find plenty of time for:

_____
_____
_____

Among focus time, play time, connecting time, physical time, down time, time in, or sleep time, these are the things I might benefit having more time for:

_____
_____
_____

Among all of the ways I spend my time, these are the things I might think about doing less of because they may not support my wellness:

_____
_____
_____

Two months from now looking back on today, here's what I wish I had started doing or persisted in doing today:

_____
_____
_____

There are lots of things I want to do in the next two months, but I can commit to doing the following specific behavior today and tomorrow so that my future self will benefit:

_____

_____

_____

Here's my list of big and small things I've done in the last two months to move toward my most meaningful, mentally healthiest life, like showing up to each TMS appointment and saying "no" to extra hours at work. (I'll add to this list over time.)

_____

_____

_____

_____

_____

_____

_____

_____

Among friends, family, coworkers and professional helpers, the following people could make up my Dream Team of Support:

_____

_____

_____

For my own balance in scheduling, I am using:

_____

_____

_____

_____

When I think about this scheduling, I notice feeling:

_____

_____

_____

My biggest obstacles to sticking with a schedule are:

_____

_____

_____

_____

When I fall off my schedule, I can give myself the following loving-kindness wish:

_____

_____

_____

_____

My values that support scheduling my time are (see values in Week Zero Notes):

_____
_____
_____

By sticking to a schedule, I will be inviting in the following thoughts, feelings, sensations and rewards:

_____
_____
_____
_____

I can share my schedule with:

_____
_____
_____

Nature Connection

Dr. Rock and Dr. Siegel include connecting with nature as an important component of connecting time. Please go outside and spend at least ten minutes just tuning in to the natural world. You can notice all the beauty and complexity you see around you and also sense yourself as part of the natural world. You are a living, breathing being, similar in many ways to all the other living, breathing beings who live outside. You grow and need water, just as plants do. You move away from threats just as all other animals do. You even heat up and cool down, just as the surface of the earth does. Sense into being a part of the natural world and notice what it arises for you.

Wise Words

"Our goals can only be reached through a vehicle of a plan, in which we must fervently believe, and upon which we must vigorously act. There is no other route to success."

—Pablo Picasso

"Breathing in, I calm body and mind. Breathing out, I smile. Dwelling in the present moment I know this is the only moment."

—Thich Nhat Hanh

TMS Week Nine

"God grant me the serenity to accept the things I cannot change; courage to change the things I can; and wisdom to know the difference."

—REINHOLD NIEBUHR, SERENITY PRAYER

Strengthening Mindfulness and Your Life

Your last TMS treatment might be this week . . . Or you might have an extended protocol to help ease additonal difficulties. Some TMS participants experience a dip in mood during this week and most recover quickly. If you notice you have had a downturn and are not bouncing back, please talk with your TMS provider about possible adjustments.

If you still are experiencing the same cloud of depression symptoms as in Week Zero, you might reflect upon which outward aspects of your life have not changed in the last nine weeks and whether any of those parts of your life are obstacles to wellness, roadblocks on your path to a meaningful life.

Is there an ongoing addictive behavior you continue to participate in that is holding your brain hostage and not allowing you to grow and change? If so, addiction is not unique to you; almost 21 million Americans struggle with at least one form of addictive behavior, yet only 10% of them receive treatment.[1] About 20% of Americans who have depression or an anxiety disorder also have a substance use disorder.[2] These patterns of human behavior demonstrate our tendency to use something to turn away from the discomfort of prolonged uncomfortable emotional states, even though in the long run, those turning-away moves cause more harm than good and certainly hinder a recovery from depression. There are many ways to get help to stop using substances, find resources at the end of this book.

There are many other obstacles besides substance use that obstruct a full recovery from depression. Some people recognize that the experience of one or more traumatic events keeps them stuck in acute stress, which perpetuates depression symptoms. There are therapists who work specifically with trauma, and techniques like Eye Movement Desensitization and Reprocessing (EMDR) that were designed to disarm the most challenging impact of traumatic experiences. If you think that trauma has impacted you, you are not alone in this either. Almost 4% of adults in the U.S. will experience Post-Traumatic Stress Disorder (PTSD) in any given year.[3] This means that each year 8 million people acquire PTSD, and those who don't resolve it are added to the aggregate of people suffering from symptoms ranging from slightly uncomfortable to totally overwhelmed. (The cloud graphic in the Introduction shows some.)

Another obstacle to progress in ridding yourself of depression can be a dynamic in a primary relationship that causes continued stress and unhappiness or that limits you from meeting your own needs adequately. You could consider seeking help from one of more than 175,000 mental health providers who work with couples and families to specifically improve that relationship. Or maybe your job or main role grants extensive strain that causes you mental suffering? Perhaps your next step is to take small moves to explore making a change in your job or in one of your roles. With help, perhaps you can address any formidable obstacles in a new and ultimately effective way.

Grief and other experiences you have little control over can also derail you from your path to a most purposeful life, keeping the cloud of depression hovering. As we covered in Week Three, a well-trained mental health provider can help you discern what you can change and how to change it to move your healing along. Our human brains don't always perceive the full 360 degree picture of our own lives and we usually benefit from a caring person with experience in listening, seeing, and supporting others while also applying some technical know-how to diminish trauma's effects on your life.

While a mindfulness practice can be a refuge into a more peaceful space inside of yourself, if you've practiced diligently on your own and sense that you want more structure for practice, you might consider joining a meditation class or group. One very popular option is the 8-week Mindfulness Based Stress Reduction (MBSR) course which was started by Dr. Jon Kabat-Zinn and his colleagues at the University of Massachusettes Medical Center. MBSR is an intensive training in mindfulness that originally targeted people with chronic health problems and now is taught to people throughout the world experiencing challenges in many areas of life. While MBSR is the most recognized program, many other classes and groups can deepen your mindfulness practice: the brain loves novelty, so perhaps trying something new like yoga, tai chi or qigong will also jump-start some energy in your recovery from depression and build mindfulness skills you'll enjoy using.

Most experts recommend near-daily participation in some wellness activity, and generally, if it feels good and doesn't have negative consequences, then by all means, make it happen. While participating in an activity in person reinforces your sense of being part of something special, at this point, there are many free online resources if that works best for you. (See Resources at the end of this book.)

Understanding

Your path has not been an easy one. For too long, you suffered from depression that muted your light, squelched your joy, and robbed you of many moments of energy and focus. Now, as you open mindfully to what is happening in the present moment, you probably have a different sense of what is possible. When you close your eyes and breathe deeply, can you sense that being with what is taking place in this moment gives you grounding into your own self? You probably realize that there will be thoughts that you'd prefer to obliterate, and uncomfortable feelings that you'd like to blast off the face of the earth; by now you likely know that this is normal human stuff. You probably also have had a chance to bring some friendly compassion to the difficult experiences and have found that helpful. You are learning and growing, and that brain is changing day by day.

Even if you are experiencing improved mood on a daily basis, the sensations in your body that you'd like to shut off will not likely just do so, and you might even perceive them as a bit more vivid now that you are paying attention. Hopefully, from the hard work you've put into your participation with this guide book and the Mindfulness Sidekick Playlist, you understand that being awake—even in the face of difficulty—is an important ingredient to mental well-being. Mindful wellness demands that you turn toward life in order to be truly awake and alive. And when you are fully awake, you are in a much better position to take the next step on your path in the direction of the values that support a life worth living.

A commitment to mindfulness challenges your very human brain's way of being, and you will make mistakes along the way. You will hurt and you will feel scared, and you will have the thought that escaping it all in the ways you used to might solve your problems. You will always have a choice about what to do in this moment, when you have that sensation/that feeling/that thought. You might choose to take good, valued action. Or you might choose autopilot. Or you might choose a behavior opposed to your values. Luckily, a new moment arrives and you'll have a fresh chance to notice what IS, and to make a move, however small, toward that goal you've been yearning for and working toward these past nine weeks: *your best life.*

See that best life now in your mind; it's in this moment, every time. So don't get too ahead of yourself with worry, dread or planning. This mistake thing, this mindless thing, this overwhelmed-with-emotion thing, this pain-and-suffering thing, these millions-of-thoughts-that-won't-stop-thing are all normal human brain experiences. And even though training the brain toward mindfulness is strenuous, you can do it anyway, *one moment at a time.* Close your eyes and be here.

Maybe you can choose one thing that's positive, that you've done well, that has gotten easier. While there are many obstacles along the way, aren't those roadblocks mostly thoughts placed there by your supposed "problem-solving brain?" Can you keep your mind focused on that one good thing you've done and grow the good? Close your eyes now and summon the positive, immerse yourself, marinate your brain in the good you've already done. And take a deep breath to let it sink in. That's it.

Joseph B. Wirthlin added to Lao Tzu's wisdom with: "A journey of a thousand miles begins with a single step. Watch your step!" and if you've made it this far in *The Mindfulness Sidekick*, you've taken *miles* of watchful steps. Now your journey continues with the next single step and a sense of the good in that mind of yours. Keep walking!

Home Practice

Notice what mindfulness practices provide you maximum benefit and take part faithfully each day. Bring an attitude of trust and patience to your moments. Be generous with yourself and others. Let go of everything—planning your desperate plans, comparing yourself to others, expecting more than you get—and rest in the refuge of the present moment when you can, like a birdwatcher waiting to see what flies near you in the forest today. When you can't muster the patience, then notice that too. If you choose to spice up your life, try a variety of practices and slather on the same attitude of generous, patient acceptance when you can.

The end of TMS treatment is an important time to check in with your therapist and support person, to be honest about what depression is like for you now and what help you'll need in future weeks to continue your best efforts. You might tune into whether the person providing support still can play a positive role for you, and if the answer is no, please find someone else to be with you on this path. Your TMS provider will certainly have recommendations for your Support Dream Team. The NOW is too vital *not* to make the most of it.

Review your schedule for a healthy mind and deal with any potential obstacles to your scheduled success. Include your support people in this process.

Writing Reflection

I have identified the following obstacles in my own recovery from depression:
___
___
___
___

Here's what I can control and what I cannot:
___
___
___
___

With the control I have, I choose to explore:
___
___
___

I'll ask for help from the following people:
___
___
___

The good I can expand is that I:

_____
_____
_____
_____

When I think about finishing treatment, I have the thought that/I notice that I feel:

_____
_____
_____
_____

I am most scared about:

_____
_____
_____

I am relating to that fear by:

_____
_____
_____
_____

I feel most excited about:

_____
_____
_____

I feel most joyful about:

_____
_____
_____

I will act on all this by:

_____
_____
_____
_____

This is different from how I used to relate because:

_____
_____
_____
_____

This contributes to my well-being because:

_____
_____
_____

TMS treatment is ending, but my wellness journey is continuing. I will fold mindfulness practice into my daily life by:

_____
_____
_____
_____

I originally chose to do TMS because:

_____
_____
_____
_____

There were some very uncomfortable parts that I made it through, including:

_____
_____
_____
_____

But I continued on because:

_____
_____
_____
_____

I learned that:

_____
_____
_____
_____

In the future, I will support my wellness journey by:

_____
_____
_____
_____

Nature Connection

Spend time each day sitting out in nature. Look above you and notice the passing clouds, remembering that your inner experiences are like those clouds, passing through the bright vastness that is awareness. Close your eyes and listen to the sounds around you, letting go of any need to control the sounds or to understand them, rather, just letting them come in to your ears. Rest in the movement of the air, in the temperature around you and in the sensations that are rising and falling within you. Notice the ways in which impermanence makes itself known in nature right now. Just as everything in nature changes moment to moment, so do the thoughts, feelings and sensations inside of you. Get to know what you can change around you and what you can just observe and be present with, and bask in any serenity therein.

Wise Words

"What is REAL?" asked the Rabbit one day, when they were lying side by side near the nursery fender, before Nana came to tidy the room. "Does it mean having things that buzz inside you and a stick-out handle?"

"Real isn't how you are made," said the Skin Horse. "It's a thing that happens to you. When a child loves you for a long, long time, not just to play with, but REALLY loves you, then you become Real."

"Does it hurt?" asked the Rabbit.

"Sometimes," said the Skin Horse, for he was always truthful. "When you are Real you don't mind being hurt."

"Does it happen all at once, like being wound up," he asked, "or bit by bit?"

"It doesn't happen all at once," said the Skin Horse. "You become. It takes a long time. That's why it doesn't happen often to people who break easily, or have sharp edges, or who have to be carefully kept.

"Generally, by the time you are Real, most of your hair has been loved off, and your eyes drop out and you get loose in the joints and very shabby. But these things don't matter at all, because once you are Real you can't be ugly, except to people who don't understand. Once you are Real you can't become unreal again. It lasts for always."

Excerpted from *The Velveteen Rabbit*, by Margery Williams

NOTES

Introduction

Find the Mindfulness Sidekick YouTube Playlist at:
https://bit.ly/MindfulnessSidekickPlaylist

1. Mindfulness Meditation can bring stress reduction: Goyal M, Singh S, Sibinga EM, Gould NF, Rowland-Seymour A, Sharma R, Berger Z, Sleicher D, Maron DD, Shihab HM, Ranasinghe PD, Linn S, Saha S, Bass EB, Haythornthwaite JA. Meditation programs for psychological stress and well-being: a systematic review and meta-analysis. JAMA Intern Med. 2014 Mar;174(3):357-68. doi: 10.1001/jamainternmed.2013.13018. PMID: 24395196; PMCID: PMC4142584.

2. Mindfulness meditation may reduce anxiety levels: Hofmann, S. G., & Gómez, A. F. (2017). Mindfulness-Based Interventions for Anxiety and Depression. *The Psychiatric clinics of North America*, 40(4), 739–749. https://doi.org/10.1016/j.psc.2017.08.008

3. Mindfulness meditation improves symptoms of depression: Goyal M, Singh S, Sibinga EM, Gould NF, Rowland-Seymour A, Sharma R, Berger Z, Sleicher D, Maron DD, Shihab HM, Ranasinghe PD, Linn S, Saha S, Bass EB, Haythornthwaite JA. Meditation programs for psychological stress and well-being: a systematic review and meta-analysis. JAMA Intern Med. 2014 Mar;174(3):357-68. doi: 10.1001/jamainternmed.2013.13018. PMID: 24395196; PMCID: PMC4142584.

4. Mindfulness meditation may also reduce depression by decreasing levels of inflammatory chemicals: Kasala ER, Bodduluru LN, Maneti Y, Thipparaboina R. Effect of meditation on neurophysiological changes in stress mediated depression. Complement Ther Clin Pract. 2014 Feb;20(1):74-80. doi: 10.1016/j.ctcp.2013.10.001. Epub 2013 Oct 18. PMID: 24439650.

5. People who did mindfulness meditatation stayed asleep longer and had improved insomnia severity: Jason C. Ong, PhD, Rachel Manber, PhD, Zindel Segal, PhD, Yinglin Xia, PhD, Shauna Shapiro, PhD, James K. Wyatt, PhD, A Randomized Controlled Trial of Mindfulness Meditation for Chronic

Insomnia, *Sleep*, Volume 37, Issue 9, 1 September 2014, Pages 1553–1563, https://doi.org/10.5665/sleep.4010

6. Trauma-Sensitive Mindfulness: Throughout our daily lives we experience discomfort inside in minor and extreme ways; we naturally react to that discomfort by moving away from it, like a cat away from fire. This moving away from discomfort is unnecessary and can become part of the problem. Instead of moving away, you can learn to stay, to bring curiosity—even wonder or awe—to whatever experience is arising and to watch what's happening without stapling a judgment to it. The application of nonjudgment allows some space to experience what's happening, and in that space you can take a new tiny step towards some aspect of a life you want to lead. Staying with an uncomfortable inner experience might be difficult but doesn't merit a judgment of "wrong" or "bad" and might give you permission to keep on going forward, being kind to yourself. So, whether you are sitting in meditation, eating something, doing a body scan, walking, doing yoga or just living your daily life, staying present is the most courageous, difficult, and healthy thing you can do for yourself.

The Mindfulness Sidekick encourages you to pay careful and constant attention to your inside experiences. This can increase traumatic stress for people who have experienced trauma, resulting in feelings of dysregulation, flashbacks or dissociation. During each mindfulness activity you try, you will always have the opening to stop what you are doing, open your eyes, look around you and ground yourself back into the safety that surrounds you in the present. For more information on how to gain safety while doing mindfulness practices, you can check out the following:

- https://www.headspace.com > blog > 2016/12/11 > med..
- https://www.mindful.org/the-science-of-how-mindfulness-relieves-post-traumatic-stress/
- https://davidtreleaven.com David Treleaven's podcast hosts many well-respected teachers discussing trauma-sensitive care in the practice of mindfulness.

TMS Week Zero

1. The nine attitudes of mindfulness: In the 1980s, Jon Kabat-Zinn, one of the grandparents of secular mindfulness practice in the United States, enumerated seven attitudes that help support mindfulness practice:

   NONJUDGMENT is the impartial witnessing of the thoughts, feelings and sensations as they arise. With nonjudgment, we can intentionally notice them with kindness, resisting the inclination to criticize either the experience or the fact that they have arisen. With nonjudgment, there is space for compassion, empathy, and connection to ourselves and others.

   PATIENCE lets happenings unfurl naturally without a need to control or rush to a desired outcome. With patience we can "stop rushing and start arriving."

   BEGINNER'S MIND is the willingness to experience all that we experience as if for the first time, with fresh curiosity. This is also called **child's mind**. In his book *Zen Mind, Beginner's Mind,* Shunryu Suzuki writes "In the beginner's mind there are many possibilities, in the expert's mind there are few." This newness brings special attention to the experience and opens us to new possibilities of understanding and action.

   TRUST is about accepting the validity of our own perceived experiences, leaning in to our inner wisdom and allowing who we are to fully arise. We can develop more objectivity and faith in our intuition. We are also allowing this mindfulness practice to lead us to deeper understanding.

   NON-STRIVING allows us to be present with what IS rather than strain to achieve a goal or desired outcome, resulting in our lack of presence on our path. When we let go of judging how far we've gone and whether that's good or bad, we can embody our values more peacefully.

   ACCEPTANCE is the acknowledgement and welcoming of experience as it is in the moment. It's not passive settling, it's recognizing things for the way they truly are. When we open to all aspects of experience we can willingly accept painful, pleasant, and neutral experiences. When we shut ourselves off from the painful experiences and only open to the pleasant, we deny part of life and miss out on the full range of emotional experiences that makes human life unique. As Karl Jung said, "what you resist persists."

LETTING GO is simply letting things be as they are without the need to try to control your thoughts, feelings or actions. Release the feeling of being trapped by your feelings of anxiety, know that the sensations in your chest are just sensations, they are not a fixed part of you, and they will pass if you let them.

Dr. Kabat-Zinn added the following two attitudes to reflect a growing awareness of their benefit on mental wellness and reduction of stress;

GRATITUDE allows us to notice the many blessings we have and distracts us from the misfortunes that we face naturally in life. When we string together instances of felt appreciation, we weave a web of gratitude that, over time, strengthens our ability to notice the good. Jon Kabat-Zinn says "There is more good than bad, more working than not working in our lives."

GENEROSITY How powerful it is to give yourself over to life and to others; it demonstrates that you care and enhances interconnectedness for you in the world. We are so often rushing off into the next thing and the giving of your own time and attention becomes a powerful gift.

Adapted from: Kabat-Zinn, Jon. *Full Catastrophe Living: Using the Wisdom of Your Body and Mind to Face Stress, Pain, and Illness.*, 2013.

See video of Dr. Kabat-Zinn on your on your Mindfulness Sidekick Playlist at https://www.YouTube.com/watch?v=2n7FOBFMvXg

TMS Week One

1. Pet Scans: Dr. Mark George, Biological Psychiatry Branch Division of Intramural Research Programs, NIMH 1993.

2. Definition of the mind from Dr. Daniel Siegel. Dr. Siegel is a Clinical Professor of Psychiatry at the UCLA School of Medicine and the founding co-director of the Mindful Awareness Research Center at UCLA. Dr. Siegel explains the mind at https://www.dailymotion.com/video/x6l6p9u and you can learn more about Dr. Siegel at https://drdansiegel.com/.

3. "You can name it to tame it," a term coined by Dr. Siegel, suggests that pairing language with our experience helps develop mental calmness, or equanimity. Here's a helpful article: https://www.mindful.org/labels-help-tame-reactive-emotions-naming/

4. Definition of sensation: https://www.merriam-webster.com/dictionary/sensation

TMS Week Three

1. Donse L, Padberg F, Sack AT, Rush AJ, Arns M. Simultaneous rTMS and psychotherapy in major depressive disorder: Clinical outcomes and predictors from a large naturalistic study. Brain Stimul. 2018 Mar-Apr;11(2):337-345. doi: 10.1016/j.brs.2017.11.004. Epub 2017 Nov 11. PMID: 29174304.

2. For more info on how to find a therapist:

    - https://www.apa.org/ptsd-guideline/patients-and-families/finding-good-therapist
    - https://www.psychologytoday.com/us/blog/finding-new-home/202001/how-find-the-right-therapist

- https://www.thecut.com/2017/12/a-beginners-guide-to-finding-the-right-therapist.html

TMS Week Four

1. Growing the good is explained at https://www.rickhanson.net/growing-good/

2. Gardner, B., Lally, P., & Wardle, J. (2012). Making health habitual: the psychology of 'habit-formation' and general practice. *The British journal of general practice : the journal of the Royal College of General Practitioners*, 62(605), 664–666. https://doi.org/10.3399/bjgp12X659466

3. Jennifer Behnke, LMHNP, practices in McMinnville, Oregon. She can be found at www.thriveintegrativepsychiatry.com

4. Toepfer, S. M., Cichy, K., & Peters, P. (2012). Letters of Gratitude: Further Evidence for Author Benefits. Journal of Happiness Studies, 13(1), 187–201. https://doi.org/10.1007/ s10902-011-9257-7

5. Rash, J. A., Matsuba, M. K., & Prkachin, K. M. (2011). Gratitude and well-being: Who benefits the most from a gratitude intervention? Applied Psychology: Health and Well-Being, 3(3), 350–369. https://doi.org/10.1111/j.1758-0854.2011.01058.x

6. Harbaugh, C. N., & Vasey, M. W. (2014). When do people benefit from gratitude practice? The Journal of Positive Psychology, 9(6), 535–546. https://doi.org/10.1080/174397 60.2014.927905

7. Jackowska, M., Brown, J., Ronaldson, A., & Steptoe, A. (2016). The impact of a brief gratitude intervention on subjective well-being, biology and sleep. Journal of Health Psychology, 21(10), 2207–17. https://doi.org/10.1177/1359105315572455

8. Homan, K. J., Sedlak, B. L., & Boyd, E. A. (2014). Gratitude buffers the adverse effect of viewing the thin ideal on body dissatisfaction. Body Image, 11(3), 245–250. https://doi. org/10.1016/j.bodyim.2014.03.005

TMS Week Five

1. Here are three resources from YouTube that might be helpful in thinking about change in the systems you are a part of as you recover from depression:

    - "Homeostasis: Why Changing Families is Hard-and How you can make change last" from Therapy in a Nutshell at https://www.YouTube.com/watch?v=fuOK3921W2M

    - "An overview of Bowen Family Systems Theory" at https://www.YouTube.com/watch?v=-GK7LaT5rxY

    - "8 Common Characteristics of a Dysfunctional Family" from Psych2Go at https://www.YouTube.com/watch?v=EkVOBhJbMj8

TMS Week Six

1. Quotation from: Rosenberg, Marshall B. *Nonviolent Communication: A Language of Life*. 3rd Ed. Encinitas, CA: PuddleDancer Press, 2003.

    See above citation, p231 and for more information, please visit www.nonviolentcommunication.com or https://www.nonviolentcommunication.com/pdf_files/4part_nvc_process.pdf

2. Go to https://www.cnvc.org/

   Helpful access to learning more: "Pocket NVC," "NVC Dialogue," and "NVConnect" are three digital apps that you might find helpful in supporting your efforts to learn and use Compassionate Communication. Some people like the lower tech version by downloading the lists available at:

   - https://www.cnvc.org/training/resource/needs-inventory
   - https://www.cnvc.org/training/resource/feelings-inventory

   Finally, if you recognize that practice will make you a better Compassionate Communicator, you can search for NVC practice groups near you.

TMS Week Seven

1. Fredrickson BL, Cohn MA, Coffey KA, Pek J, Finkel SM. Open hearts build lives: positive emotions, induced through loving-kindness meditation, build consequential personal resources. J Pers Soc Psychol. 2008 Nov;95(5):1045-1062. doi: 10.1037/a0013262. PMID: 18954193; PMCID: PMC3156028.Z

2. Kearney DJ, Malte CA, McManus C, Martinez ME, Felleman B, Simpson TL. Loving-kindness meditation for posttraumatic stress disorder: a pilot study. J Trauma Stress. 2013 Aug;26(4):426-34. doi: 10.1002/jts.21832. Epub 2013 Jul 25. PMID: 23893519.

3. Galante J, Galante I, Bekkers MJ, Gallacher J. Effect of kindness-based meditation on health and well-being: a systematic review and meta-analysis. J Consult Clin Psychol. 2014 Dec;82(6):1101-14. doi: 10.1037/a0037249. Epub 2014 Jun 30. PMID: 24979314.

4. Jazaieri, H., Jinpa, G.T., McGonigal, K. *et al.* Enhancing Compassion: A Randomized Controlled Trial of a Compassion Cultivation Training Program. *J Happiness Stud* 14, 1113–1126 (2013). https://doi.org/10.1007/s10902-012-9373-z

5. Shahar B, Szsepsenwol O, Zilcha-Mano S, Haim N, Zamir O, Levi-Yeshuvi S, Levit-Binnun N. A wait-list randomized controlled trial of loving-kindness meditation programme for self-criticism. Clin Psychol Psychother. 2015 Jul-Aug;22(4):346-56. doi: 10.1002/cpp.1893. Epub 2014 Mar 16. PMID: 24633992.

6. https://jackkornfield.com/meditation-loving-kindness/

TMS Week Eight

1. *The Healthy Mind Platter for Optimal Brain Matter.* Copyright © 2011 David Rock and Daniel J. Siegel, M.D. All rights reserved. Used with permission. https://drdansiegel.com

2. To search for a free printable daily page planner check out:

    - https://daydesigner.com/collections/printable-library
    - https://andreadekker.com/my-daily-routine-free-printables/
    - https://scatteredsquirrel.com/2019/07/simple-daily-planner-printables/

Healthy Mind Plan for _____
_{date}

What I want to remember/tell myself in order to support myself:_____
_____
_____

Healthy Mind Ingredients:

Physical Time: Exercise, Movement, Physical work	Focus Time: On/Offline School Work	Downtime: Relaxation, Entertainment, >50% off screens	Time In: Quiet Brain Breaks, Screen-free	Play Time: Spontaneous, joyful experiences	Connecting: Contact with other living beings and nature	Sleep Time: In Slumber

Start with the scheduling items that are non-negotiable, add in the times you'll need for focus time to accomplish your school, work or family goals and then fill in the rest of the schedule with the other times to make a mind-healthy day.

Healthy Mind Ingredient	Time	Event/Activity/Task
	Morning	
	Noon	
	Evening	

What did I do well today that deserves my gratitude?_____
_____

What did I let go of so that I could embrace a healthier mind state?_____
_____

TMS Week Nine

1. https://www.aamc.org/news-insights/21-million-americans-suffer-addiction-just-3000-physicians-are-specially-trained-treat-them

2. https://adaa.org/understanding-anxiety/co-occurring-disorders/substance-abuse#:~:text=About%2020%20percent%20of%20Americans,an%20anxiety%20or%20mood%20disorder.

3. https://www.therecoveryvillage.com/mental-health/ptsd/related/ptsd-statistics/#:~:text=Prevalence%20of%20PTSD&text=Overall%2C%20PTSD%20affects%20around%203.5,Americans%2C%20in%20a%20given%20year.

RESOURCES

Great Books:

- Brach, Tara. *Radical Acceptance: Embracing Your Life with the Heart of a Buddha*. New York: Bantam Books, 2004.
- Chödrön, Pema. *When Things Fall Apart: Heart Advice for Difficult Times*. Boston: Shambhala, 2000.
- Germer, Chris K., *The Mindful Path to Self-Compassion: Freeing Yourself from Destructive Thoughts and Emotions*. New York: The Guilford Press, 2009.
- Hanson, Rick, and Forrest Hanson. *Resilient: How to Grow an Unshakable Core of Calm, Strength, and Happiness*, New York: Harmony Books, 2018.
- Hanson, Rick. *Hardwiring Happiness: The New Brain Science of Contentment, Calm, and Confidence*. Westminister, MD: Random House Audio, 2013.
- Harris, Dan. *Meditation for Fidgety Skeptics: A 10% Happier How-to Book*. New York: Spiegel & Grau, 2018.
- Harris, Russ. *The Happiness Trap*. New York: Constable & Robinson, 2014.
- Kabat-Zinn, Jon. *Wherever You Go, There You Are: Mindfulness Meditation in Everyday Life*. New York: Hyperion, 1994.
- Neff, Kristin. *Self-Compassion : The Proven Power of Being Kind to Yourself*. New York: William Morrow, 2011.
- Rosenberg, Marshall B. *Nonviolent Communication: A Language of Life*. Encinitas, CA: PuddleDancer Press, 2003.
- Siegel, Daniel J., *Mindsight : The New Science of Personal Transformation*. New York: Bantam Books, 2010.
- Singer, Michael A. *The Untethered Soul: The Journey Beyond Yourself*. Oakland, CA: New Harbinger Publications, 2007.
- Stahl, Bob, and Elisha Goldstein. *A Mindfulness-Based Stress Reduction Workbook*. Oakland, CA: New Harbinger Publications, 2010.

Great Mindfulness Teachers:

Jack Kornfield, PhD. is an author, Buddhist practitioner, Spirit Rock Meditation Center founding teacher, and one of the key teachers to introduce Buddhist mindfulness practice to the West. He is especially known for his teaching of the cultivation of loving-kindness. He has published books such as *A Path With Heart* and *The Art of Forgiveness, Loving-Kindness and Peace*. He hosts a podcast called "Heart Wisdom." https://jackkornfield.com/

Jon Kabat-Zinn, MD, Ph.D. is internationally known for his work as a scientist, writer, and meditation teacher engaged in bringing mindfulness into the mainstream of medicine and society. He founded the Mindfulness-Based Stress Reduction Clinic, and the Center for Mindfulness in Medicine, Health Care, and Society. Dr. Kabat-Zinn is the author of two best-selling books: *Full Catastrophe Living: Using the Wisdom of Your Body and Mind to Face Stress, Pain and Illness* and *Wherever You Go, There You Are: Mindfulness Meditation in Everyday Life*. https://www.mindfulnesscds.com/pages/about-the-author

Lama Rod Owens, a Lama in the Kagyu School of Tibetan Buddhism, has published *Love and Rage: The Path of Liberation Through Anger* and *Radical Dharma: Talking Race, Love and Liberation*, which he co-authored with Reverend angel kyodo williams and Jasmine Syedullah Ph.D. Lama Rod speaks, teaches and writes about the topics we often are afraid to talk about: race, gender, sexuality, and identity. https://www.lamarod.com/

Reverend angel kyodo williams, a Black, mixed-race Zen priest, teaches the buddhist dharma through a lens of society, change, love, and justice toward liberation. She wrote *Being Black: Zen and the Art of Living With Fearlessness and Grace*, and co-authored, with Lama Rod Owens and Jasmine Syedullah Ph.D., *Radical Dharma: Talking Race, Love, and Liberation*. https://angelkyodowilliams.com/

Rick Hanson, PhD., a psychologist spreading the good word about the science of positive brain change, has published many books, including *Hardwiring Happiness* and *Buddha's Brain*, and has lots of free offerings on his website, including a regular weekly meditation, and a podcast called Being Well. https://www.rickhanson.net/

Tara Brach, PhD., writer of *Radical Acceptance: True Refuge and Radical Compassion,* is a psychotherapist and meditation teacher. She shares a weekly guided meditation and talk that blend Western psychology and Eastern spiritual practices. She teaches about using mindfulness meditation and self-compassion in relieving emotional suffering, serving spiritual awakening and bringing healing to our world. https://www.tarabrach.com/

Resources for Help with Depression:

https://www.mentalhealth.gov/

"MentalHealth.gov provides one-stop access to U.S. government mental health and mental health problems information . . . aims to educate and guide the general public, health and emergency preparedness professionals, policy makers, government and business leaders, school systems, local communities."

https://www.nami.org/Home

"NAMI, the National Alliance on Mental Illness, is the nation's largest grassroots mental health organization dedicated to building better lives for the millions of Americans affected by mental illness."

https://suicidepreventionlifeline.org/

"The National Suicide Prevention Lifeline is a national network of local crisis centers that provides free and confidential emotional support to people in suicidal crisis or emotional distress 24 hours a day, 7 days a week. We're committed to improving crisis services and advancing suicide prevention by empowering individuals, advancing professional best practices, and building awareness."

Addiction Recovery Resources:

- A list of resources from the U.S. Department of Health and Human Services:
  https://www.samhsa.gov/find-help/national-helpline

- A list from the National Association of State Alcohol and Drug Abuse Directors:
  https://nasadad.org/treatment-recovery-resources/

- National Eating Disorders Association (NEDA):
  https://www.nationaleatingdisorders.org/substance-abuse-and-eating-disorders

- National Council on Problem Gambling:
  https://www.ncpgambling.org/programs-resources/

- The Addiction Center has many resources on its website:
  https://www.addictioncenter.com/community/porn-addiction-hotlines-resources/

Mindfulness Programs:

www.Palousemindfulness.com

This online MBSR training course is 100% free, created by a fully certified MBSR instructor, and is based on the program founded by Jon Kabat-Zinn

You can also google "Mindfulness-Based Stress Reduction" and your town or region to find an MBSR teacher near you.

Other Helpful Resources:

- David Treleaven, PhD. on Trauma-Sensitive Mindfulness: https://www.davidtreleaven.com/
- Russ Harris teaches an online program to go with his wonderful book, *The Happiness Trap:* https://www.thehappinesstrap.com

Acknowledgments

My heart is full of gratitude for the folks that helped me, from seeding the first idea through to the fruit you've just feasted on.

My partner, Silas, who is endlessly and enthusiastically supportive of me and my work. What a blessing to have someone who believes in me and is always ready for a consult.

Jennifer Behnke, PMHNP, sister change-maker, for encouraging this partnership and for inspiring me to walk the path to my own richest, most purposeful and joyful professional life.

My colleagues and dear friends, Natalie Bowker LMFT, and Kimberly Wasserman, LCSW for encouraging me along the way and reading parts of the manuscript.

R.M.S., for providing important early feedback on the experience of TMS. You have been a brave soul who has inspired me to pay close attention.

Tim Buckley, for bringing his depth of understanding and experience to the reading of Week Six about Compassionate Communication.

Sarah Lahay, of C'est Beau Designs, who did a wonderful job designing this book and walking me through the design and production process with patience, grace and true skill.

My dear and diligent proofreaders: my mom, Cynthia Steiner, my son, Metolius and my friend, Jennifer Johns. Thank you all for your focus and clever stewardship of the English language! You three are amazing!

Andra Kovacs for in-the-clutch back cover help and supportive magical energy along the way.

The McMinnville Monday Mindfulness Community, for their enduring enthusiasm for learning and their willingness to open their hearts and be present in love. May the sunlight always stream in.

My most helpful mindfulness teachers along the way, Susan Woods and Robert Beatty for their enduring wisdom and ability to open me to what I needed at the time.

Seed teachers Jon Kabat-Zinn, Tara Brach, Rick Hanson, Lama Rod Owens, Pema Chodron and Kristin Neff for providing amazing examples of brilliance and mindful compassion. They are the hikers before me that teach me where the path to a most meaningful life lies.

My children, Ukiah and Metolius, for their hilarious skepticism and unending love and affection. I do this for them, and for all children, young and old, who deserve to deeply understand that they are good, that they are whole and that they deserve the entire universe in the wide expanse of their minds as well as the deepest roots into this beautiful and fragile earth.

May we know our best selves and give our best selves to the earth and to all living beings.

Wingspan Farm and Forest, McMinnville, Oregon
April 2021

About the Author

Amy Halloran-Steiner is a psychotherapist and mindfulness teacher who has spent over 25 years connecting people with themselves, with one another, and with the earth. Over the years, she has used her creative energy to bring traditional therapy and wellness practices to more unconventional settings, making projects come alive and wellness be accessible to a greater variety of people. Some of her diverse work has included: leading teens in wilderness treatment, supporting bilingual elementary school kids and families, counseling university students, connecting groups and individuals with nature, guiding children and adults in yoga and mindfulness and tending space for healing alliances with therapy clients.

Amy lives on a farm at the edge of a forest in the Willamette Valley in Oregon with her husband, where they raise vegetables and fruits, trees and animals, and two vibrant teenagers. A student and steward of wild spaces, she spends her time away from the farm hiking, traveling and swimming in the ocean and beloved desert canyon rivers. She hopes this book might offer the same connective appreciation she has for each client she has worked with, and she dedicates its benefits to all humans.

www.ingramcontent.com/pod-product-compliance
Lightning Source LLC
Chambersburg PA
CBHW081506080526
44589CB00017B/2666